THE EVOLUTION OF CAPITALISM

THE EVOLUTION OF CAPITALISM

COMMERCIAL TRUSTS

THE GROWTH AND RIGHTS OF AGGREGATED CAPITAL

BY

JOHN R. DOS PASSOS

ARNO PRESS
A NEW YORK TIMES COMPANY
New York • 1972

Reprint Edition 1972 by Arno Press Inc.

Reprinted from a copy in
The State Historical Society of Wisconsin Library

The Evolution of Capitalism
ISBN for complete set: 0-405-04110-1
See last pages of this volume for titles.

Manufactured in the United States of America

- - - - - - - - - - - - -

Library of Congress Cataloging in Publication Data

Dos Passos, John Randolph, 1844-1917.
Commercial trusts.

(The Evolution of capitalism)
Original ed. issued as no. 97 of Questions of the day series.
1. Trusts, Industrial--U. S.--Law. I. Title.
II. Series. III. Series: Questions of the day.
New York, Putnam.
KF1649.3.D6 1972 338.8'5 77-38275
ISBN 0-405-04118-7

Commercial Trusts

THE GROWTH AND RIGHTS OF AGGREGATED CAPITAL

AN ARGUMENT DELIVERED BEFORE THE INDUSTRIAL
COMMISSION AT WASHINGTON, D.C.
DECEMBER 12, 1899
CORRECTED AND REVISED

BY

JOHN R. DOS PASSOS

OF THE NEW YORK BAR

AUTHOR OF "STOCK BROKERS AND STOCK EXCHANGES"
"THE INTERSTATE COMMERCE ACT," ETC., ETC.

G. P. PUTNAM'S SONS
NEW YORK & LONDON
The Knickerbocker Press
1901

"QUESTIONS OF THE DAY" SERIES.

The Knickerbocker Press, New York

ANALYSIS OF CONTENTS

Contents

INTRODUCTION

LARGE aggregations of capital, concentrated in the hands of corporations, are called "trusts." In form, the difference between a corporation possessing a large, and another a small, capital is, however, only one of degree; but in principle the difference may be very deep and important, and lead to grave results.

The Courts of this country, applying the old and effete rules of monopoly or public policy, have almost unanimously declared these so-called "trusts" illegal. But in the contest between the technical principles of law and the progress of trade the law has succumbed, and the trusts have multiplied with great rapidity.

Whether the operations of natural laws will be a sufficient check on these mammoth commercial consolidations for the protection of the people; or whether it is necessary to regulate them by express legislation; behold the problem!

The argument which is herewith presented to the public was delivered before the Industrial Commission, at Washington, December 12, 1899. I claim for it the merit of frankness and independence of thought and expression.

The growth and development of these colossal combinations of trade demand constant and close attention.

A few years' more experience with them will show whether they are good or evil, to the laborer, the producer, the manufacturer, the purchaser. In the meantime the discussion is going on; and in the hope that my views may throw some light upon the subject, I have presumed to give them greater publicity.

JOHN R. DOS PASSOS.

NEW YORK, October, 1901.

COMMERCIAL TRUSTS

COMMERCIAL TRUSTS

MR. CHAIRMAN AND GENTLEMEN OF THE COMMISSION:

I APPEAR before you this morning to make some observations upon the legal and historical aspect of the question of the aggregation of capital; whether that capital be represented in money, in goods or in labor. Because of its immaturity, I am here to endeavor to rescue this subject from the domain of law, where it does not belong, and to place it in the field of speculation and thought and political economy, where it does belong.

Preliminary Remarks.

I appear here as the representative of no corporation, of no aggregated interest or of no individual, and the opinions and views which I shall have the honor to express are entirely my own; I alone am responsible for them. They are made without consultation with anybody, and whatever criticism may arise from the observations which I shall address to you must therefore fall upon me alone.

I congratulate the country that this great and interesting, not to say absorbing, question has fallen at last into a legitimate place of discussion, and that this Commission, composed of individuals chosen from all the walks of life, is to sit and to hear everything that anybody wishes to say, and to report its conclusions upon the facts in shape for definite action. I regard it as of the greatest importance to this country that questions of this kind should primarily pass through the ordeal of a Commission. If they are left exclusively in the hands of politicians, very much is said of an extravagant, emotional and sensational character, and the results which accrue from such a method of inquiry and examination are in a general way unsatisfactory to the reasonable, thinking people, and to the important business interests of the country. Whatever is filtered through this Commission, I believe, after its exhaustive and laborious study of the questions involved, will be of service to the whole country.

Another observation in respect to this Commission which, it seems to me, I should be remiss if I did not allude to. It is not often that I am in the position to praise legislation; but I can commend the statute by virtue of which you occupy your official positions here, not only in its substance, but as to the language used therein. Certainly the language of the act under which you are appointed, and are working, is most admirable. It is brief, and charges you with the examination of the two great propositions that arise out of this important subject, namely:

"§ 2. It shall be the duty of this Commission to investigate questions pertaining to immigration, to labor, to agriculture, to manufacturing and to business, and to report to Congress and to suggest such legislation as it may deem best upon these subjects."

"It shall furnish such information and suggest such laws as may be made a basis for uniform legislation by the various States of the Union, in order to harmonize conflicting interests, and to be equitable to the laborer, the employer, the producer and the consumer."

Hasty and Ill-considered Legislation Deprecated.

Yet, is not this act an extraordinary commentary upon the way laws are made in this great country, which we, in moments of admiration and enthusiasm, are prone to call the leading nation of the world, in its civilization, in its progress and in all the elements which make up a great nation? Is it not a remarkable comment upon that civilization and upon our methods of legislation that nine or ten years after a law has been passed by the Congress of the United States, a Commission is created for the purpose of inquiring whether any laws are necessary upon that particular subject? Making the laws first, and inquiring into their necessity afterwards! Plutarch states that a Locrian who submitted legislation stood up in the temple with a rope around his neck, prepared to be strangled, if his proposed law was not adopted.* Would such a prospect discourage a modern legislator with a new speech to deliver and a new project to propose?

I say to you to-day, not in any spirit of sensationalism, but from a sincere belief and conviction, that if the laws could be piled together, in some place capable of holding them—the laws which have been enacted since 1848, when, under the guise of law reform, ill-considered codification was introduced into this country and a weed thus planted in our judicial and legal system, which has overgrown and hidden from view the real and simple purposes of justice and law—I say that the man who could put a match to this accumulation of verbiage, duplication and multiplicity of laws and let them burn, is entitled to a monument at the hands of the American people for ridding

* The Epizephrian or Italian Locrians. See Grote, Vol. III., 510.

them of statutes and useless books, and bringing them back to a condition where simplicity and science would go hand in hand towards producing satisfactory and prompt judicial results.

Let me make one more preliminary observation before going into the questions which I shall discuss. When public matters are discussed in this country, the great question, or the great cry, rather, always is "legislation," "legislation," "we want more laws," and the inquiry is pushed in that line, until each political party is in a race to outdo the other in making statutes—and this is called legislation; and these statutory enactments are made in order to appease what they consider to be the predominating sentiment of the hour. In this aspect one party is no worse than the other. They are both the same; in the general method of treating public questions, and in their superficial mode of legislation.

Now, it is necessary for me to remind you of what is involved in legislation. Proper

The Theory and Object of Legislation Explained.

legislation requires that before a statute is passed by the law-making body its subject-matter should be thoroughly understood. We must, in order to have complete and thorough legislation, go back to the basis of the social organization; and no legislation can be satisfactory unless it is examined in that aspect. You must understand the relation that a citizen occupies to the Government before you can legislate, and you must be fully convinced that legislation is necessary.

These views are elementary and academic, but it is necessary to treat questions of this description in that way in order that we may arrive at a proper result; and I ask you this morning to go back to the supposed origin and basis of political society to discover whether any additional legislation is needed.

No one can trace back to its origin, human society; but we all have defined views upon the subject, and the deductions of writers like Montesquieu and Burlamaqui, and others, who have paid attention to questions of the spirit and nature of laws, are generally accepted.

When a man is born into the world, it is assumed that he bargains with some government for citizenship; that is the accepted origin of society. He says to the government, "I will give you my allegiance, I will give you my fealty, in return for protection," which organized society, a necessary condition of human existence, accepts, and affords him and his property protection. This is a crude description of the social compact.

Now, what does this compact mean? It is called political or civil liberty; which a celebrated authority defines to be "the natural liberty, so far restrained by human laws (and no further) as is necessary and expedient for the general advantage of the public." Here is a distinct and clear contract, on the part of the government, not to intrude upon, or molest, the natural liberty of man, except in cases of plain and paramount necessity.

Now, mark you. Every law that you make is, as it were, a nail in the coffin of natural liberty. The object of government is not to make laws; the object of government is to avoid making laws—the very reverse to-day of a legislator's habits. And no law should be made, which looks to the combined interests of the citizen and the government, unless these primary principles are adhered to. First, you must be convinced that a real necessity requires a law to be made. You must examine into the causes; you must know the mischief that you seek to avoid or prevent, before your hand takes the pen to write a law which takes away the natural liberty of mankind.

If these principles were only thought of, and all questions, which were to be the subjects of law, should be impartially and thoroughly considered, much unnecessary legislation would be avoided, and the condition of this country, so far as its legal affairs are concerned, would be very much better.

Gentlemen, but one more word preliminarily to the main subject, which I shall now touch.

Before we discuss any subject, it is necessary that we should understand each other as to terms; we should agree as to the issue involved—the primary matter which we are brought together to consider, and hence, there is a necessity to have a definition. A definition is an absolute prelude, a *sine qua non*, to a proper discussion of any subject, whether it is legal, moral, religious or otherwise, because without definitions men can never get together in an argument or agree as to the point involved. They cannot understand each other.

Definition of a "Trust."

Mr. Locke, the great philosopher, has remarked that half the disputes which separate mankind have arisen simply from a neglect to define terms and premises.

Now, there is the word "Trusts," used in the discussion of the question of aggregated capital, and that word is heard so frequently, in this country, that it has become a term for aggregated capital—has become a phrase, representing all of the forms of combined capital.

We must exclude from this discussion words and phrases that are useless and meaningless, or we can make no intelligent progress. A "trust," in its legal sense, according to Judge Story, an authority on equity jurisprudence, is an equitable interest which a man has in personal or real property; and the history of trusts, if anybody is disposed to go back to study the origin of them, will be found to have arisen out of an evasion of some of the principles of the feudal law. But, in the sense in which the term "trust" has been used, so far as it has been technically and legally used, for the last two hundred years, it means, as Judge Story has said, an equitable right in personal or real property. That is, it assumes, that the trustee, who is the person controlling, or the physical custodian of the corpus of, the real or personal property, is the legal owner, while the person really interested is called the *cestui que trust*, or the beneficiary. He, the latter, is the actual owner. The trustee is the one given the legal title, but he has no duty, except to carry out the terms of the trust, whereas the actual owner is the beneficiary; and although the title is not in him, he can call upon the trustee at any time, according to the terms of the trust instrument, to account for and fulfil the mission of the trust.

Meaning, History and Object of "Trusts."

In applying that word "Trust" to the question of aggregated capital, about which I shall speak, it means this: assume that certain persons, called a syndicate, desire to become the owners of some manufacturing business, or commercial enterprise which is owned by, say, six corporations; having bought the shares of these companies, they get together and they make what is called a trust deed, or a trust agreement. That trust agreement recites the terms under which the securities are held; that is, the stock, the shares of these six constituent companies, are taken and placed in the hands of a trustee, who has no actual or real ownership, except that he is the custodian—the shares belong, accordingly, to the trustee, to administer the trust. That was the object of a trust, so far as it applied to the modern aggregation of capital. Let me try to make this subject perfectly clear. All of the stock of the six corporations is deposited with, say, one person, and that person issues receipts, called trust certificates, by which the persons receiving the trust certificates are entitled to a defined interest, as therein stated, in the properties of those six companies, whose shares have been lodged with the trustee.

A trust was not a novel proposition, when it was recently introduced into dealings for the control of certain businesses. It was the application of an old principle of law to new conditions. The object of it was this: to keep people, who had no business to know, from discovering the secrets of that trust, and of the business which it controlled. That is the object of a trust (a perfectly innocent, and a perfectly laudable object, in my estimation). If persons interested in a certain business had formed one corporation and put the six constituent companies into one corporate body, it would have been heralded to the world, and all persons would have had the right to go into the County Clerk's office, or the office of some officer, entitled and authorized to receive those papers, and to look at them; the object of the creation of the trust was to avoid that publicity, and therefore they had a trust agreement, which was deposited in the safe of the trustee, and nobody knew anything about it, except the beneficiaries—that is, the persons holding the trust certificates.

Now, if the learned Chairman here had an interest in one of these companies, he would have received a stock or a trust certificate, and that trust certificate would have entitled him to have received, at the proper time, dividends, if any were earned, and ultimately to receive his proportion of the principal. That would have been the interest of the holder.

The beneficiary, or the *cestui que trust*, or holder of the trust certificate, had at all times, the right to walk into a court of equity, and demand, that all of the business, conducted by the trust, should be laid open to him and that all information pertaining to it should be accessible to his inquiries. As to him, therefore, there was no secrecy beyond what he chose to allow; as to the general public, there was secrecy—such secrecy as is incident to and necessary in the transaction of any business, private or corporate.

The only two large industrial corporations which resorted to that system, which I will call ancient procedure and ancient law, were the Standard Oil and the Sugar Trust. Through the enforced decrees of courts, which declared such trusts monopolies and against public policy, they gave up the *form* of trusts, and they assumed the *form* of corporations, and when the Sugar Trust divested itself of this exterior garment, and when the Standard Oil Company divested itself of its exterior garment, known as a trust, it did not affect the vital body, it did not affect the corpus; it did not affect the real, substantial objects involved in the trust, but they simply put on other suits of clothes, and appeared in the community in the new garments.

As Burke says,*

"While you are discussing fashion, the fashion is gone by. The very same vice assumes a new body. The spirit transmigrates, and far from losing its principle of life by the change in its appearance, it is renovated in its new organs with the fresh vigor of juvenile activity. It walks abroad; it continues its ravages whilst you are gibbeting the carcass, or demolishing the tomb."

So the word "trust" may be made to disappear and in fact has been discarded in the discussion of these questions, now and for-

* *Reflections on the Revolution in France*, Vol. V., p. 259.

ever; because the courts have set their seal of condemnation upon that *form* of consolidation, and they require that people who have in view the aggregation of capital shall now consummate it through the instrumentality of a corporation; and in discussing these questions we must dismiss this word "trust" as meaningless and useless.

Of course, I have been speaking of the mere *form* which the transaction assumed. In *substance* this bringing together of businesses was intended to avoid competition—to save useless expenses; and in most cases the *real object* of the consolidation was to control the particular business involved by concentrating it under one management.

Objections to Aggregations of Capital Considered.

We then arrive at the question as to what was the meaning and intent of Congress in the appointment of this Commission; and what is the meaning and intent, of the public discussion, which has gone on from one end of this country to the other, upon the question of aggregated capital. It means, so far as I comprehend the question—and I want to state it as broadly as possible, so that not even the most dilettante critic can find fault with the statement—that certain organizations, or certain people, or certain writers, contend that the aggregation of capital, or aggregations of business, is pernicious or detrimental to the public welfare, and the public good, and they therefore ask this Commission, as they have asked the courts, under the legislation which is already existing, to come forward and help to forever stifle this alleged evil.

They say all "big businesses" are bad; but "small ones" are all right. The same class of critics caused an author to make the ironical rhyme:

"To steal for pence is paltry and mean,
To rob for millions with a soul serene
Soils not the hands: all success is clean."

Now gentlemen, I want you to observe, that the advocates of legislation against aggregated capital, have not, even at this late day—years after the agitation has been commenced—put their views into definite form; and there is the difficulty in discussing the question. Let me try to give to their vague theories a "local habitation and a name." Let me strive to make a postulate, for the people who oppose aggregated capital, that will form a basis of discussion—historic, moral, legal or religious, if you please. Let me create an issue.

Should Amount of Capital Employed in any Business be Limited?

Aggregated capital is wrong, is pernicious, is fraught with danger! What is meant by that? There are three things that must be looked into in approaching this question; namely, (1) the *amount* of capital intended, (2) the *person* in whose hands the capital is vested, and (3) the *use* to which the capital may be put.

Now, let us follow this arrangement and see whether there is any intelligent basis made by these advocates, and I will put them all in one class—newspapers, political organizations, writers and everybody else; is there any intelligent or sufficient information vouchsafed, which covers these three important points?

First, the *amount* of the *capital*; second, the *person* who is to use the same; and third, the *use* to which the capital is to be put.

Now, let us see, as to the amount of the capital. How much capital is pernicious? Is a million dollars capital, aggregated into the hands of a corporation, pernicious; or is two millions; or is five millions; or is ten millions; or is fifty millions; or is a hundred millions?

You cannot discuss questions of proposed legislation unless you have fixed principles, and information, to go by. You, sitting here as intelligent inquirers into the truth, going to the bottom of things, must have facts. You cannot predicate legislation upon doubt and uncertainty. You must be able to know and say how much aggregated capital is pernicious; whether it is a million dollars, or five million dollars, or twenty millions, or fifty millions, or a hundred millions. Which amount is it?

Those who oppose aggregated capital have never yet, so far as my observations are concerned, or so far as my research has gone, answered that question intelligently, or answered it at all. In fact, that is a problem which this body is left to solve upon mere hypothesis.

Can Amount Controlled by Corporations be Limited?

Then the second one; the *person* in whom the capital is vested. Are one hundred millions of dollars more pernicious in the hands of a corporation than in the hands of a partnership; are fifty millions of dollars more pernicious in the hands of a partnership than in the hands of an individual? Will the opponents of aggregated capital make answer to these questions to this Commission?

Are you prepared to say, gentlemen, that you will allow an individual in this community to have a hundred million dollars, but will deny the same right to a corporation? Now, let us see where that will lead you to. Let us follow this question down to a legitimate business result, and that is all I ask.

Do not let us wander into the realm of speculative discussion; because I am here to meet serious objections, not flimsy hypotheses. Are you prepared to say that you will give an individual the right to hold one hundred million dollars, and that you will deny the same privilege to a corporation? Now, let us see where such a conclusion would lead to.

The capital of a corporation is divided into many parts—shares and bonds, or one or both. The corporation capital is not generally owned by one person; it is usually owned by many persons; there are frequently as many as ten thousand shareholders in one corporation—ten thousand shareholders or bondholders of small capital and small means, who put their money into an organized concern for the purpose of reaping a reasonable rate of interest through the instrumentality of dividends, and in a belief that the aggregation might result in something profitable. Now, suppose you deny ten thousand people the right to participate in aggregated capital, and you afford that right to one individual, who can congregate in his hands that vast and enormous sum of money. Would that be just or logical? I am giving no expression of my own humble opinion about these questions; I am simply opening up this subject, and showing you how difficult your mission is: to propose laws in the absence of such vital knowledge.

Should the Uses of Capital be Restricted?

Very well; now, let us go another step, third; what is the *use* to which the money can be put? Is it pernicious that a hundred million dollars should be invested in railroads? Is it pernicious that a hundred million dollars should be invested in transportation, canal companies, insurance companies, banks and real estate; is that what the opponents of capital claim? We have no light on this question. Has anybody been so bold as to appear before this honorable Commission to advocate laws which were calculated, as they say, to choke to death this modern monster, called "aggregated capital," without giving some information upon this point? Has anybody come before this Commission and given it data which will enable a reasonable mind to come to an honest conclusion in respect to the *use* to which capital should be limited? Will you say that a corporation cannot put a hundred million dollars in the organization of a manufacturing business; will you say that it shall not put a hundred million dollars in real estate; will you say that a corporation formed in New York, with a hundred million dollars, for the purpose of irrigating lands in Texas, or in Arizona, is illegal, and at the same time allow a hundred million dollars, to go into the banking business, or into the insurance business? Where is the line of demarcation to be drawn; where will you begin with the chalk, as Mr. Burke says, and mark the boundary that separates the pernicious from the commendable, or proper, employment of capital?

These vital points are not answered, so far as I have been able to learn, and they must be answered before you can make any intelligent law; and the reason—and I shall approach that hereafter—why the repressive laws against aggregated capital have not been executed is that they never were comprehensibly studied by the legislators, and the subjects never properly discussed or understood; but the legislators madly dashed to the work, threw ink upon paper and called it legislation, and they ask the Courts to enforce it—enforce a statute based upon doubt, and guess, and speculation, and against the natural laws of trade and business.

Now, let me again try to formulate some postulate for these opponents of capital. They say that aggregated capital, held by a corporation, for the purpose of manufacturing, or business, or commerce, is pernicious and detrimental to public interests. I cannot undertake to give the language which has been used by some of the orators in portraying the dreadful future which is in store for this country if aggregated capital is permitted to exist. But adopting the proposition most frequently used that "aggregated capital in the hands of corporations is detrimental to the interests of society," I ask on what grounds?

It is said that aggregated capital is pernicious, because it creates a monopoly, and, therefore, we must advance one step further in the discussion and try to discover what a monopoly is. Definitions, as before mentioned, are the essentials that you gentlemen want and must demand; they are like the guides on a perilous road at night, when you see the white stones marking the route to enable you to safely pilot your way. But if you allow yourselves to drift about in a sea of speculation, without any compass or chart, without any definite notion of where you are going, you will most likely land upon the rocks and be shipwrecked. Therefore, arguing this matter as a lawyer, I look upon definitions as of vital primary importance.

Does Aggregated Capital Create a Monopoly?

Now, the word "monopoly" has a legal, it has a grammatical, and it has a historical meaning. The legal and grammatical meaning of the word "monopoly" is the same. A monopoly, according to the dictionary, is the exclusive privilege of traffic— "the exclusive possession of anything as a commodity or a market." It is an exclusive privilege, resting in the hands of one person or corporation, to the exclusion of everybody else, and to comprehend a monopoly you must realize that there can exist no monopoly, unless it is exclusive. That is the whole basis of it. This word monopoly received a significance, and a great emphasis, in the time of Elizabeth. She gave out, as Hume will tell you—and I am not going into that part of history, except to refer to it, so that if anybody wishes to pursue the subject he can do so—Hume tells us that Queen Elizabeth gave out these exclusive monopolies to various courtiers, in return for favors, or for services, often otherwise unrewarded. The Queen paid in that way instead of with money. She did not incorporate commercial companies; they were not heard of, not thought of, not dreamed of

Definition of "Monopoly."

in her time; but she took John Smith or John Jones, as the case might be, and she said, "Hereafter, you are to have the exclusive privilege of manufacturing or selling tobacco in the Kingdom of England, and nobody else can do it"; and every dictionary will tell you that such a transaction illustrates the meaning of monopoly.

We lawyers, brought up on the milk of Blackstone, absorbed a prejudice against monopolies, to such an extent, that when you mention monopoly to a lawyer, it is precisely like waving a red flag before a bull. It is a fundamental basis of a lawyer's education to oppose monopolies. But there have existed in this Republic, with but few exceptions, to which I shall refer, no monopolies since its organization, and therefore the use of the word monopoly, in the legal and in the grammatical sense, must be discarded from this discussion; it has no business here; it has no technical or practical meaning when applied to aggregated capital.

But there are two monopolies which may

still exist. There is a monopoly in patents. The people of the United States have seen fit to say that when a man invents a process, which goes through the ordeal of the Patent Office, and is regarded as being a practical invention, Congress can give him the privilege, for seventeen years, of using it, for his own sole and exclusive benefit.

In all their furious denunciations, in all the extreme criticisms to which the opponents of aggregated capital have gone, I have not seen any suggestion that we should repeal the patent laws. So, that if some one were to discover a process, by which he could make a loaf of bread out of a stone, for one cent, and every baker and miller in the world would be ruined thereby, there is not one voice, which could effectually be raised against the granting of such a patent. And yet the patentee would, Jove-like, armed with the thunder of his patent, have in his hands, all that tremendous power, directly from the Government of the United States itself, and before which power, the monopolies granted by Queen Elizabeth, to her favorite courtiers, would sink into absolute insignificance.

That is one kind of monopoly that exists; and in your deliberations, gentlemen, you must very carefully weigh this question; as to how far, you can restrict the use of capital in the aggregated form, on the one side; and, at the same time allow these extraordinary patents, becoming more and more extensive, as science advances, to be issued by the government, on the other.

There is still another species of monopoly, and that is a monopoly in the form of a special charter granted by a legislature, or by the national government. Here is a monopoly in a certain sense. But it is of no great importance in this discussion, because, by force of constitutional provisions, every special charter which has been granted within the last—I should say twenty-five or thirty years—I do not want to be put down as if I were actually accurate, but within the last twenty-five or thirty years—I think every State Constitution has given the legislature absolute authority, to peremptorily revoke charters, so that no great detriment can occur to the community, through their instrumentality. And, as a matter of fact, almost every State, if not all, has laws which enable individuals to become incorporated companies, through its general laws; and it is unnecessary to apply to the legislatures for special charters, except in extraordinary cases, and only when special circumstances seem to disclose a peculiar merit in the enterprise. So, there is nothing to call for special remark about special charters.

We come, therefore, to the consideration of another kind of monopoly—one growing out of existing conditions, and the meaning of which one cannot find in his dictionary; and we must discard legal, grammatical and historical monopolies from this part of the discussion. Driven out of the position that aggregated capital is a technical monopoly, its opponents have assumed to create another and a new one, and there has been created, what I shall call a *resulting* monopoly, a monopoly *in fact*, and that I would define to be this: that while aggregated capital, or individual wealth, or partnership wealth, has not sought through the instrumentality of a license, or a special prerogative, from the government, to exercise certain privileges, to the exclusion of all other people, yet the influence of concentrated wealth is so great, that it amounts to a virtual monopoly. This is a monopoly *in fact*: a monopoly which *results* from the condition of existing things. Now, that is the monopoly with which we have to deal, and which you have to discuss, and about which you have to undertake to legislate. That is a monopoly in fact, a new monopoly, not alluded to by any legal writers, so far as I remember, or so far as I have been able to find, but a new meaning to the word "monopoly" which has grown out of the modern aggregation of capital, and it is claimed, that if the aggregation of corporate capital is accomplishing the same thing as a technical monopoly, it ought to be suppressed.

This brings me to another proposition, which is this: that the necessities for the use of large sums of money—of combined capital are the natural result of commercial and financial conditions; not only the natural but the necessary result of existing conditions. I claim, that aggregated capital is the necessary and natural handmaid of advancing commerce; and that without it we could never have attained our present colossal industrial development.

History of Rise and Growth of Aggregated Capital.

Now, I shall endeavor to prove my proposition in this way: I am going to show you the history of capital; and the *forms* which it has from time to time assumed to meet enlarged and advancing commercial conditions.

I shall not talk at random. I shall refer to actual facts, and speak by the card of history. If history is wrong; if we cannot consult it with any degree of safety, then all of my argument must fall to the ground, and the fabric, which I am endeavoring to raise here, must crumble into dust.

The question of partnership is the one which I will first discuss. The communion **Partnerships.** of goods among two or three or more men can be found clearly and satisfactorily in the ancient world. You will find that in ancient Greece among that people there existed what was called a communion of goods. Two or more men figured, that their individual efforts would be made more satisfactory, by a combination—putting their goods together, and they formed what was called the communion of goods; that is the equivalent of the Greek word in English, "communion." Partnerships existed, and held their way down, through the various gradations of history and society, until we reach our English history; from whence we draw all that is of great importance in our laws and our customs, and institutions, and in fact almost everything else of value, in our national life. These partnerships answered their purpose, as long as they were found to be fit and proper instrumentalities; and when they did not, why, something else was discovered. A partnership was all very well,. so long as it could furnish means for advancing mercantile and commercial affairs; but you can see at once, when I explain the disadvantages of partnerships, that when we began to develop and unfold this colossal country (and this development is alone answerable for all the alleged sins of aggregated capital), when we entered upon very large business affairs, partnerships would not answer.

There were three distinct characteristics in every general partnership. In the first place, each partner was liable for the debts; that fact circumscribed its operations and utility. John Jones and John Smith entered into a partnership, and John Smith was answerable, for all the debts; so that John Smith might have put a hundred thousand dollars into the partnership, and John Jones would bring the firm in debt to the amount of five hundred thousand dollars, and John Smith was liable; that was one of the disadvantages of partnership.

Another disadvantage was this: that when one of the partners died, the business was at an end. Death dissolved the partnership, just as it does marriage, and although the firm might have been in the midst of a flourishing business, the death of one of the partners immediately cancelled it, stopped it and prostrated the business.

Of course, I remember that lawyers have undertaken to provide for the continuation of a partnership after the death of one or more of the partners, but about this attempt at continuation, the average man argues in this wise: "Well, I don't want to continue it after my death; I shall have a widow and children" and all that; and there were innumerable difficulties, that you gentlemen understand yourselves from practical experience. When you undertook to grapple with the problems which an advancing American commerce opened, with the limited means and many disadvantages of partnership, that form would not answer at all.

Then there was another element against

the partnership; and that is that you could not bring a suit against the partnership without suing all of the parties; which was very disadvantageous; you could not sue one partner only for a partnership debt. It was necessary to join them all, and serve them all, if you wanted an individual judgment. These disadvantages, and the increasing demands of commerce required us to advance a step further and find other and broader and greater means for transacting business.

In Pennsylvania, I think, the first step was taken towards the introduction of a new and expanded system of capital, and it was called a "limited partnership." These partnerships were originally drawn from the customs and laws of Italy, and then transplanted into France, where they were known under the name of *en Commandite*, and they were subsequently introduced into the United States.

Limited Partnership.

Let me explain what a limited partnership was. I do not mean that you do not know; but I want to explain it as a part of this discussion. A limited partnership was a method, by which a man entering into a commercial, or manufacturing business, could limit his liability. If two individuals wished to enter into a partnership, and one did not want to engage in active business, he could advance, say, $100,000 to his associate, who was the general partner, and escape a liability, by filing a certificate in the proper clerk's office, that he was a special partner, and making a publication in the newspapers, and having it put on the sign, that he was a special partner. The result of which was, that he was enabled to engage in a business without individual liability, beyond the sum that he advanced in the inception of the enterprise, and the whole responsibility was thrown on the general partner.

Now, in France, and in Pennsylvania also, to a certain extent, I believe, they allowed *shares*—certificates of stock—to be issued against the interest of the partners, so that this partnership became a *quasi*-corporation. The limited partnership only existed for the time mentioned in the articles of copartnership; but the interest of each partner might be segregated into shares and negotiated in the form of certificates of stock. They allowed them to be issued, very largely, in France, and there were some very extensive litigations there, which you will find recorded in Troubat (*Law of Limited Partnership*), if you have a desire to investigate the subject. Yet, you can see, that the system of limited copartnership, furnished but a very meagre contribution to the advancing wants of commerce.

Commercial Corporations.

The ingenuity of the age was great enough for the occasion, and out of those necessities there came the commercial corporation. The commercial corporation, as it exists to-day, was never developed in any substantial form, in this country, previous to the year 1850.

You will find that the first book on corporations was published in 1793 by Kyd. But it was altogether limited to questions of municipal corporations; and if you take the books of Watkins and Grant on corporations, and all the other literature on corporations, you will find that up to, and even in, the first American book of Angel & Ames, which was published in 1831, there is hardly an allusion to our commercial corporations; and it was not until after 1850, when commercial corporations came in vogue, that one discovers any legal literature upon this subject. The first general corporation act, in the State of New York, was passed in 1848; it was known as the Manufacturing Act.

When the railroad system of the country was introduced and began to be used, we discover that the commercial and manufacturing corporations gradually came into vogue, the one following closely in the wake of the other; and through the instrumentality of general laws, three or four, or ten or twelve, or any number of persons beyond three, might get together, and file a certificate, and become a corporation. The tendency of legislation was at first to narrow the limits of a corporation; that is, in the amount of capital which it was allowed to have; and you will find, if you consult the law, that in almost every instance previous to 1861, when the war broke out, the several States placed limitations upon the amount of corporate capital. That restriction gradually disappeared, until to-day, in most of the States, in almost all of what we call the commercial States, there is an unlimited amount of capital allowed; so that several individuals may now get together, and form a corporation, and do business, with an unlimited capital.

Nature and Functions of Corporations.

Now, one of the most important elements in the discussion of this question of aggregated capital, is to understand what a corporation is, and, therefore, I come to another definition. I will take Blackstone's: "A corporation is an artificial person created for preserving in perpetual succession certain rights, which, being conferred on natural persons only, would fail in the process of time."

Let us see what the essence of a corporation is, and how capital and business shifted from a general partnership at first, into a limited partnership, and from a limited partnership into a corporation. Take the legal history of partnerships, limited partnerships and corporations, on the one side; take the history of commercial expansion; take the history of territorial expansion; take the history of railroad expansion, on the other, and you will see what necessary aids they were to each other, and how, as railroads and commerce expanded; how, as new territories and fields were opened, our manufacturing industries increased and enlarged, and how capital, like an apt and willing handmaid, kept apace with all; how, in the colossal development of this country, capital, both in substance and form, was always ready to supply the vital means, to feed the modern Titan of business in its most stalwart growth.

A corporation has certain functions impossible to be exercised by individuals or partnerships.

First, it has perpetual succession. That is, its existence is unbroken and uninterrupted, down to the time when it is to expire by limitation. You can now incorporate a company for a thousand years, if you wish, or fifty, which is the period generally followed. A corporation may consist of a thousand individuals; many of them have more than that number; to-day the New York Central, and the Pennsylvania railroads have many thousand stockholders. They die; their descendants die, but the corporation is undying. It goes on forever. This result a copartnership could not accomplish; neither a general nor a limited one.

What is the second? The second quality of a corporation is, that a stockholder is not liable for the debts of the corporation. This was, therefore, as one can see, the most attractive form of carrying on business. It enables several individuals to go into a business, and to put in five or ten or fifteen, one hundred thousand dollars, or any other sum, and each knows the limit of his liability. This was the feature that appealed to business men. They knew, that when they went into a corporate enterprise, their responsibilities were limited and fixed, which could not be the result in a partnership where the liability was unlimited.

Another feature of corporations which was of the highest importance, was the transmutability of the stockholders' interests, the power of disposing of their stock in the corporation. They could sell or transfer their interests in the corporation to others. Every contributor to the capital stock of a corporation receives a certificate of stock; that certificate of stock he can put in his drawer or safe; it is personal property, and he can sell it in the markets or give it to his children. It is always there in a tangible, neat and easy form, for him to use; it is a certificate that he has an interest in the corporation and that his liability was fixed by that certificate of stock. This could not be done in a copartnership. A sale could not be made of his interest in such a business, because it was based upon personal and peculiar reasons. In the development of large enterprises, certainly nothing could be happier, than the conception of a corporation; certainly, nothing could be better. The men who originally went into them, who were the pioneers, in the formation of our commercial and our manufacturing corporations, and our railroad corporations, and our insurance corporations, who have all long since passed away, were shrewd, bright and skilful merchants. In adopting this system of business, men were enabled to sleep peaceably; it enabled each man to limit his liability; it enabled him to have his certificate of ownership in his pocket, and enabled the corporation itself, which was an entity, a legal entity, to carry on a great enterprise, without any regard to who the stockholders were, or whether they were dead or alive, except as they contributed to its success by choosing proper boards of directors and officers to manage its concerns.

Now, in regard to the capitalization. The originators raised the capital, by issuing shares of stock and bonds. The money needed for their business was raised by selling the stock to whomsoever would buy it—a few or many.

The Method of Raising Capital by Corporation Bonds and Shares Explained.

In this connection, I have to speak about a subject of the utmost importance in this discussion and in its effect upon your opinions and labors—something that I regard as one of the greatest and cleverest devices ever created by man to collect, aggregate and distribute capital. I allude to corporation mortgages, by which thousands of persons poured their money contributions, small or large, through various channels, into the common treasury of the company; all the vast capital necessary to run these great enterprises being contributed through the sale of mortgage bonds until the full capital demanded by a particular business project was supplied.

If you will reflect upon the subject, it becomes plain that there is no individual who is capable of loaning a very great amount of money on mortgage to a corporation, or in a word, to make one large individual loan.

If it were possible for him to do it, it would not be good policy, and the largest mortgage, I think, that has ever been created, the highest individual mortgage in the United States, was not greater than four million dollars, and that money was loaned on real estate, I think, in New York, by one of the large insurance companies. A man with four or five million dollars, or with twenty or thirty million dollars, does not care to put that amount of money, as a loan, in one place, on one piece of property: as they say, "it is putting too many eggs in one basket." He might loan to the extent of a million; probably he would go to two millions, but when you get up to four or five millions, it is too great for an individual loan.

Large enterprises require immense sums of money to finance and run them. Twenty, thirty or fifty millions cannot be furnished by one or two men. Such sums are supplied from numerous private pocket-books —from hundreds or thousands of contributors, as the circumstances demand.

Now see what the ingenuity of man has accomplished, and an American, too; because I believe that the first railroad bonds, secured by mortgage, emanated from Philadelphia. It is necessary to know what a railroad, or corporation, mortgage is, and how it is managed. A company makes a mortgage, say, for fifty million dollars, on its property to a trustee to secure many bonds usually of the denomination of $1000. Who would, or could, advance fifty millions of dollars, in one transaction? Why, the wealth of the Astors, the Vanderbilts, the Rockefellers and Pierpont Morgan, and all those men whose wealth has now become the subject of common talk, and is spoken of every day, as being so colossal; even the combined wealth of all of these men would be but a drop in the bucket, as it were, if they should undertake to carry out, without other aid, the gigantic corporation enterprises developed in this country. Hence, they create a corporation mortgage, which secures bonds; one mortgage of, say, $100,-

000,000; you will find plenty of them now; and bonds are made, sold and distributed all over, some amount in your hands, another amount in his, ten thousand dollars here and ten thousand dollars there, and thus through a thousand rivulets or sources is poured from all sides into a common treasury, the capital necessary to begin and continue the operations of the corporation; and through that instrumentality—of a railroad bond, or a corporation bond—all this colossal capital is raised, which enables us to carry on these railroad, industrial and commercial enterprises: using the money of the many, and not of the few. This is the great modern method of raising money for private, or public purposes. When profit is made it is divided among many; and when a loss occurs it is so divided that it falls heavily only upon a few. Thus the money of hundreds of thousands of individuals is used to develop and sustain the great industrial, financial and railroad enterprises of the country.

I do not overlook, of course, the immense

sums of money raised by the sale of preferred and common stocks. Millions upon millions of dollars have flowed into the treasuries of different companies from this source. But it is the speculative side of corporate financing. The investing and more secure side is made through the purchase of bonds secured by a mortgage.

In this connection, I wish to say a few words on the subject of over-capitalization.

Over-capitalization. The capital of a corporation is the fund or means provided for transacting the business for which the company is organized. There are two methods of capitalization: First, there is a capitalization based upon the actual value of property, and, second, a capitalization based upon the earning power; these are the two bases. You will find two classes of economists or financiers in this country—one in favor of the former method, and one in favor of the latter. They both have their adherents. I confess that I am in some doubt about the matter, because so many arguments can be made in particular cases that prevent the adoption of any uniform rule; and with the experience that I have had in creating corporations, and in putting them in legal shape, I have no opinion defined, certain and fixed upon the question as to how the capitalization should be based; because each case presents peculiar circumstances, which absolutely make it impossible to adopt an unvarying rule. If you capitalize a property for what it is worth, a manufacturing business, or a railroad business, you first employ appraisers, who will enable you to fix its value; assume that they appraise its value at fifty million dollars, the sum is fixed as the capital. Now, on the other hand, you have a property that is worth only five million dollars, but by what is called its good-will or its earning power, and trade-marks, or individual skill, and so forth, it yields more net profits than the property of fifty million dollars. You, gentlemen, have seen that illustrated in your daily business lives.

In the one case you have a property worth fifty million dollars, and its yearly earnings are, say, only two per cent., or one million of dollars. On the other hand you have a property worth only five millions of dollars, which earns twenty per cent., or one million of dollars per year.

Now, how shall these two interests be capitalized? Some are disposed to fix an arbitrary principle or rule by which capitalization is to be predicated upon the actual value, and there is to be no water. But, as you can see, that rule will work manifest injustice in many cases. Well, it is so easy for men to get up and make statements on a political platform; they are under no obligations to anybody, but their consciences; and the consciences of politicians during election times are very elastic; they find no difficulty in cutting themselves loose from history, facts and experience, and they lay down propositions which in their responsible moments they would shrink from. The truth is that the capitalization of every company must largely rest upon the peculiar circumstances which surround it. No fixed invariable rule can be made.

The question of the capitalization of corporations is a serious one, as it affects the public as well as the individual stockholders or creditors of each company. The success of all corporations depends upon what they sell to the consumer, or what they make from the traveller or shipper. If a corporation is grossly or unfairly over-capitalized, to earn interest and dividends it must charge proportionately higher prices. These the public must pay. It accordingly follows, as a general rule, that the lower the capitalization the less the tariff of charges the public must pay, because each concern ought to be satisfied with paying its shareholders a fair dividend. But a corporation may be capitalized at a small figure and pay enormous dividends, when the result to the public is the same, whether the capitalization is high or low, because the same amount of net profit is made each year. A corporation which is capitalized at $100,000,000 can pay 25 per cent. to its stockholders if its net yearly income is $25,000,000; or it can capitalize at $500,000,000 and pay 5 per cent. In the first case its stock would sell for $500 a share, and in the second it would sell for $100. The result to the public would be the same in either case, and consequently the question of over-capitalization would not solve the problem in which they are interested, viz.: in not paying more than the goods or service were worth. Out of this branch of the subject will arise great questions for future legislators to solve; first, can and ought the profits of these corporations to be limited? and second, if yea, how can this be legally and fairly accomplished? The law fixes the rate of interest which lenders may receive. It has been asked, can the same rule be applied to corporations or aggregated capital? I warn you that this is dangerous ground to tread upon. It is full of mires and quicksands. Yet there is no problem which a legislator cannot solve, if he enters upon the inquiry in a proper spirit: a determination to be just to capital and fair to the public.

As yet this field is unexplored. We have nothing, so far, but ignorant and wholesale denunciation of "trusts," without any intelligent or honest effort on the part of the politicians to go to the bottom of the subject and bring to the surface the true underlying principles which should govern us in treating capital.

Much complaint has been made against over-capitalization of railroads. It is as true as gospel that many of them are largely over-capitalized. And they can be duplicated for less money. But each railroad in this country has its own history. Some of these railroads were partially subsidized by the government—the Pacific roads, for example, but most of these vast trans-continental lines, which make it possible for us to reach California and the Far West in a very short period, were built by English capital; and when I say English capital, I mean the financiering was done through the English houses, with their

German and other foreign connections; but it was not American capital; we did not have the money; and we could not build the railroads.

Now, sirs, as you sit in judgment upon these railroads, you must remember the contemporaneous history which surrounded them. Now that the roads are built; now that the country is developed; now that you have these flourishing cities all over the continent growing larger every day, it is very easy to forget the past; but when you speak of the enormous capital of the railroads, the enormous capital of these trans-continental lines, remember how they were built, and tell me if there was any other method of building these roads, than the plan adopted by the railroad builders, or contractors of this country, situated as they were at these times? And what was their situation? For example, twenty-five or thirty years ago, if a syndicate proposed to build a line from New York to Chicago, or from Chicago to San Francisco, or to New Orleans, or wherever your imagination will lead you; how were they to raise the money? Not from the government. It was not the policy of this government to give the money. The banks would not lend you the money: if for no other reason, at those times they did not have it. It was raised by private subscription. And how could they get the money? What did they do? They had to go around with an engineer's map, and with the estimated earnings that were to be produced from the operations of the road. And how did they approach capital? Would I come to you, sir, as a capitalist and say, "Will you take ten thousand of these bonds at par?"—bonds on an incompleted road, which you did not know would earn one dollar of interest or not. No, sir. Put yourself in the position of the railroad contractors of this country when you are talking about inflated railroad capital, and see how the inflation could have been avoided. What did they do? Why, they offered a hundred shares of common stock as a bonus, or some other bonus, and they sold the bonds at fifty, and sixty, and forty, or whatever they could get for them. And there was no other way of doing the business. And unless they had sold the bonds your country would not have been developed. And millions of dollars were lost upon bonds which only cost thirty or forty cents on the dollar, because the development of the country was not then fast enough to enable the pioneer roads to earn their full interest. Of course, times have changed, and the marvellous rapidity of our growth has brought the country at last up to this originally inflated capital, and roads which were a few years ago hopelessly bankrupt are now earning full interest upon their bonds and paying large returns upon their stock. There is an undoubted evil attendant upon all over-capitalization; but if the railroads, as their volume of business increases, will reduce the passenger and freight rates, the evil will be at least measurably overcome. If they do not, it is the duty of the various legislative bodies to take the matter into their own hands and fix rates and charges. But under any circumstances we must never forget the part played by our first railroads in the opening and development of this marvellous republic.

I am not defending inflation. I am giving you the facts, and I am showing you that there was no possibility of money being raised, except through the instrumentality of these large bonuses. Well, many of these railroads that were given away almost, have now reached a success, far beyond the dreams of their most sanguine founders; they have been reorganized, and recapitalized again, and are paying handsome profits on each investment. The development of the country has been so phenomenal, the business has been so enormous, that people who invested in these securities have amassed colossal fortunes. If you take engineers, and go over the tracks of the New York Central and Pennsylvania Railroad; why, they may tell you they can build the roads for less money than the sums at which they are capitalized. Perhaps this is true. But it could not have been done at the time the roads were first built; nor can a railroad be built to-day upon an actual hard-cash basis. You can project a railroad line from one point of this country to another, but you cannot get people to invest money in it, when it is new and undeveloped, unless there are extraordinary temptations to them. You will not put your money into a railroad that has not been built, and pay par for the bonds, even if they carry six per cent. interest.

I think the above furnishes some explanation of the origin, the accretion and the development of capital; I have given you an outline of the history of it from its beginning down to the present time.

Do Aggregations of Capital Create Monopolies?

I come, then, to the gist of the subject, and that is the question whether these corporations for manufacturing, commercial or industrial purposes create monopolies, and if they do, whether any and what laws are necessary to be made to restrain or destroy them. I have shown you their development. And I claim, as a matter of law, that they are not technical monopolies. I maintain that unless you license and give exclusive and superior privileges to a corporation it is not a monopoly. You may perhaps put your hand upon one or two corporations—large, gigantic corporations—in this country that to-day are monopolies in fact. Have they been given exclusive and superior facilities and privileges to accomplish that result? Have they received privileges which are denied to other people? Are they thriving upon any National or State law which protects them as against others in the same business class? Are they the possessors of franchises through the instrumentality of contracts with railroad companies, which are denied to others? If they are, a law which would put everybody on an equality—and that is what people want—would not, in my judgment, be wrong. If any corporation in this country occupies a superior position, stands on a higher eminence as to privileges than any other corporation, or any other body of men, the privileges which belong to it should be taken away. Corporations, partnerships or individuals, as to their business or commercial or legal rights, must be placed upon an absolute equality. I do not know what has transpired before this Commission. You may have evidence in your possession which shows that discriminations have been made; that discriminations exist. If they do, why, I think it is within your province to suggest some remedy.

Now the next question is, does the present condition of aggregated capital demand that it should be stifled, or restricted or curtailed by laws, National or State?

I have two or three propositions upon this question of monopoly in fact or resulting monopoly. They are not mere theories of political economy, but are based upon facts—because I do not intend to enter into the sphere of political economy in this discussion; it is not my province. The province of a lawyer is to keep to the facts as far as it is possible, and

Should Aggregated Capital be Regulated by Legislation?

that is what I am trying to do. A law based upon theory or hypothesis can be nothing but an experiment.

First: I claim that the natural laws of trade form a sufficient barrier to prevent or break up most commercial monopolies. That, I say, is not a proposition of political economy; it is a proposition of fact, which I shall prove, otherwise it is entitled to no weight. Every effort—and I know of several within my own knowledge—that has been made to "corner" an article of commerce has failed. You remember the pools in wheat and corn. Two colossal attempts to corner the breadstuffs of the world were made in very recent years; and you know the result. Men can choke the arteries of commerce for the time being, but the natural stream of trade will soon overflow their plans, and even when they think they are in possession of the supreme power, the laws of trade are taking it away from them.

Before you undertake, therefore, to legislate against monopolies, be sure that you have defined what a monopoly is, and be sure that you do not overlook the historical facts, which show that every attempt ever made to corner or monopolize breadstuffs or any other article of commerce, of this or any other country, has failed, and reacted upon its authors, and they have been ruined. Leave the natural laws of trade alone, and they will take care of themselves. You may be in the hands of a monopolistic power for a little while, but the revulsion will come. If you make general laws, aimed to strike at a single and isolated case, you do more harm to the community than a temporary monopoly would, formed by bad men, with the evil design to throttle the commerce of the country. "Hard cases make bad law."

Second: There is another principle to which I invite your attention in regard to monopolies—that whenever business is conducted in such a way as to cease to be conservative it becomes a mark for other capitalists, and the legislator can leave it alone to the outside world to take care of.

Do I make myself plain? Here is, say, a vast manufacturing corporation, with a capital of fifty million dollars, and it owns every business of the kind in which it is engaged. If the managers undertake, with all that power in their hands, to depart from conservative principles—if they undertake to raise prices to an unusual height, the outside capital which is always watching an opportunity to cngage in lucrative business will respond. That reserve capital is invited into the field, and you have the competition, which the opponents of aggregated capital regard as essential to just business conditions. Take one—perhaps the most remarkable instance of this view—the so-called "sugar trust." It owned pretty much everything when it started, and what was the result? First one refinery and then another sprang up, until you find a bitter and deadly fight and competition going on which must satisfy the bitterest opponents of aggregated capital. Will not new refineries spring up, and is it not impossible to keep them from springing up? The more that are absorbed, the greater their capital is inflated, and the more powerful are the motives to establish rival plants. Do you want laws to effect results which nature brings about so well? While you are thinking of making statutes, the natural laws of trade are silently working and pulling things to pieces. I am constantly reminded of the compactness and strength of the Standard Oil Company. I admit that good management, brains and skill have kept it compact and strong; but it has not yet run its full course. If it is a monster of oppression, wipe it out. But remember, when you attempt to regulate manufacturing corporations by statutes, that you are legislating, not against their leaders, who can take care of themselves, but against the thousand innocent people who constitute their stockholders. To attack any of these great industrial bodies to-day means the destruction of the property of the innocent masses, and not of the millionaires.

Again, industrial aggregations need no

legislation to-day. It is a question whether they have not already run their full course.

Their creation is temporarily stopped at least by natural conditions. Can you raise money to-day for these industrials? No. Why? Because the market is overcharged with them. The boa-constrictor of speculation is gorged, and until he has digested what he has already swallowed he can take no more food, no matter how tempting and luscious.

Legislate! Why, you may as well undertake to regulate the tide of the Potomac River as to fix by principles of law the rules of supply and demand which operate in regard to monopoly. Keep a stringent money market, as it is to-day, and you will have no more industrials built on old lines. You will become *functus officio* by virtue of natural conditions. Your Commission will cease to be necessary by virtue of the very laws of trade which you are asked to guide and control.

"Every European Government which has legislated much respecting the loss of trade has acted as if its main object were to suppress the trade and ruin the traders. Instead of leaving the natural industry to take its own course it has been troubled by an interminable series of regulations, all intended for its good and all inflicting serious harm." * "By their laws against usury they have increased usury." (*Ibid.*)

Not that I wish to see you go out of existence; I would continue you and your successors, forever. A commission of inquiry is the instrumentality that stands between extravagant and demagogic demands and good, sensible business judgment and the true interests of the people; it is the tribunal through which every question of currency or interstate commerce and other great public subjects should pass. Conclusions filtered through such a source must be based upon facts and not speculations; and when laws are framed after such study the people will not see any Sherman anti-Trust Acts, or

* Buckle, p. 201.

multitudes of other laws, unexecuted upon the statute books, and which make the law a by-word and a reproach. The inability of courts to carry out such statutes and give them effect is because they are not based on any reasonable or sensible principle of legislation.

Again, nor do you, gentlemen, want to interfere with combinations of capital, made successful by ability, skill and good business judgment. If a corporation, through good management of its directors, without violating any law, either moral, religious or civil, is able to reach success in business, you don't want to be urged on by feelings of envy, passion or prejudice to cut it down or to uproot it. If you find, in considering this question, that the combination of skill and good judgment in business has brought about a successful result, I say all things prompt you to encourage it rather than to discourage it, and if you can do nothing better you should let it alone.

It is not true business judgment to pull

down industrial structures at the bidding of a few—shall I call them speculative politicians?—who have no actual business experience, who have no accurate knowledge of the laws of finance, economy or commerce, but whose whole stock-in-trade consists of a pack of vituperative epithets and a string of generalities, which they use to encourage demagogism among the masses of the people.

Masses Own the Corporations.

Another consideration in connection with these industrials is entirely overlooked by their opponents. It is assumed in all of their discussions that these large companies are owned by a few capitalists. This is absolutely incorrect. They are owned by thousands of people in all stations of life—from the most opulent rich man to the prudent poor man with a few hundred dollars laid by. Examine the stock lists of these so-called "trusts" and see the names which they disclose, covering persons in all occupations and all classes of life. Their shares are open to all; any one who desires can purchase them and become a member of these corporations. Don't fail to observe that there is a difference between fighting a promoter and banker and destroying the property of thousands of innocent purchasers. When an industrial is launched a new régime is inaugurated. It must stand or fall by natural conditions. As it is economically managed; as it is properly organized; as it is conservatively capitalized, so will it succeed or fail.

The gaming-table is as reliable an investment as money placed in commercial companies where sound business principles do not prevail.

Permit me in this connection to show the futility of legislation made against the natural laws of trade or business by some historical precedents.

I maintain that all laws that have been made to prevent combinations of labor, to prevent combinations of manufactures, to prevent combinations in produce or breadstuffs, or to prevent what I may in a word call the free and unlimited exercise of commercial relations, or speculation in cereals or stocks, have been ineffectual and abortive, every one of them, and I challenge any one to point out to me in English or American history any statutes which have been passed to prevent these combinations, that have proved effective. And the simple reason is, that the laws of trade, the natural laws of commercial relations, defy human legislation; and that is all there is in it. Wherever the two clash, the statute law must go down before the operations of those natural laws. I could begin back as far as the reign of the Edwards in English history, and trace the statutes that have been passed against combinations of labor, against the combinations of the owners of produce, combinations of purchasers of or dealers in breadstuffs, and I can show you that in every instance these laws have been abortive. Whoever has the desire can find plenty of these instances in history. I will select a few

Historical and Legal Precedents that Legislation cannot Control Natural Laws.

examples to show the truth and foundation of my remarks.

FIRST.—Laws against forestalling, etc.

The offence of forestalling was described by statute, passed in the reign of Edward VI., to be the buying or contracting for any merchandise or victual, coming in the way to market, or dissuading persons from bringing their goods or provisions there, or persuading them to enhance the price when there; any of which practices makes the market dearer to the fair trader.

Regrating was described by the same statute to be the buying of corn or other dead victual in any market, and selling it again in the same market, or within four miles of the place. This was supposed to enhance the price of provisions, as every successive seller must have a successive profit!

Engrossing was the getting into one's possession, or buying up, large quantities of corn or other dead victuals, with intent to sell them again. These offences are all described in Blackstone's Commentaries, and are thoroughly familiar to the legal profession. In respect to the offence of engrossing, that author says: "This must, of course, be injurious to the public, by putting it in the power of one or two rich men to raise the price of provisions at their own discretion." Sir William Blackstone should have lived to see the results of some corners in wheat. His sympathy would have been extended, not to the consumer, but to the rich men who attempted to play with the fire of cereal speculation, and who came out of the ordeal so singed and depleted as to be unrecognizable.

All the statutes of Edward VI. in regard to regrators, forestallers and engrossers, as well as many other similar statutes which infringed upon the freedom of commerce, were repealed in 1772 as detrimental to trade by a statute of George III., the preamble and substance of which are shown in the following extract:

"Whereas, it hath been found by experience that the restraints laid by several statutes upon the dealing in corn, meal, flour, cattle and sundry other sorts of victuals, *by preventing a free trade in said commodities, have a tendency to discourage the growth and to enhance the price of the same,* which statutes, if put into execution, would bring great distress upon the inhabitants of many parts of this kingdom, * * * be it therefore enacted that an act made in the third and fourth year of King Edward the Sixth, entitled an act for the buying and selling of butter and cheese; and also an act made in the fifth and sixth year of King Edward the Sixth, entitled an act against regrators, forestallers and engrossers; and also an act made in the third year of Philip and Mary, entitled an act for keeping milch kine, and for breeding and rearing of calves; and also an act made in the fifth year of Queen Elizabeth, entitled an act touching badgers of corn and drovers of cattle to be licensed; and also an act made in the fifteenth year of King Charles the Second, entitled an act to prevent the selling of live, fat cattle by butchers; and so much of an act made in the fifth year of Queen Anne, entitled an act for continuing the laws therein mentioned relating to the poor, and to the buying and selling of cattle in Smithfield, and for suppressing of piracy, as relates to butchers selling cattle alive or dead within the cities of London and Westminster, or within ten miles thereof; and all the acts made for the better enforcement of the same *being detrimental to the supply of the laboring and manufacturing poor of this kind shall be*, and the same are hereby declared to be, repealed."

And in this connection, I beg to call your attention to what was known as the "Bubble Act," which was passed in the reign of George the First.* The "Bubble Act" grew out of the South Sea speculation, and in some aspects it was one of the most remarkable instances of speculation in the world, almost outrivalling Law's famous French scheme. The "Bubble Act" was passed about 1718, and it undertook to prevent a *recurrence of the losses* to the English nation sustained through the South Sea Bubble. The horses having escaped, the wise legislators cautiously closed the stable doors. I won't stop to explain what the South Sea Bubble was. You, gentlemen, know, or if you do not, it is easy to find a history of it in any ordinary library. But the statute, the "Bubble Act," was passed to prevent prospectuses being issued of a kind

* 9 East's Reports, p. 517.

which would seduce capital into speculation. It was supposed that so many people had lost money through the instrumentality of these prospectuses, which were gotten up in the most glaring form, that it was necessary to have legislation, and they passed that law of George the First, in which they made it a crime for anybody to print and publish or circulate any descriptions of enterprises for the purpose of alluring capital to subscribe. That statute remained in existence more than a hundred years; I think it was repealed in 1837. And thus another monument was erected to warn legislators how vain it is to endeavor to furnish brains to the community, to keep the public from being entrapped or deceived by the wiles of speculation.

There was but one application made to the Court under it, and that was made to Lord Ellenborough in 1808. The Attorney-General, at the solicitation of a private person, asked the Court for an information, which is a criminal process in the nature of an indictment, issuing at the instance of the

Attorney-General. It seemed in that case that the "promoters" of the enterprise were endeavoring to raise money to float the "London Paper Manufacturing Company," a concern that would answer to what they now call the "Paper Trust," and also the "London Distillery Company for making and rectifying genuine British spirits," which would answer to the present combination properly called the "Whiskey Trust." These were perfectly legal occupations, and perfectly legitimate industrial enterprises; but the prospectuses were contrary to the "Bubble Act," and some person, prompted by feelings of malice or envy or what not, some illegitimate influence operating upon him, applied to the Court to put in operation that statute eighty-seven years after it had been passed. It had never once been heard of; had become a dead-letter statute, and Lord Ellenborough said substantially, "Well, the people of this country have forgotten all about the existence of that statute, and the complainant comes into Court in such a peculiar position that I will not grant him any relief"; and that was the last that was ever heard of that statute, but out of this great South Sea Bubble was built a lighthouse to warn the unwary and innocent against the shoals of speculation.

The crime that the defendants in that case were charged with was this: They claimed in the prospectus that every person who subscribed to the capital would get a share which was transferable, and thus relieve himself from all liability beyond the amount of his subscription; and as there was no corporation act in England at that time, the representation was false, because they were all partners, and that was the basis on which an application was made to the Court. An act which would now be recognized as perfectly legal, if not meritorious, was then by hasty, ill-conceived legislation made a heinous crime.

This case, in 1808, illustrates that the stage of commercial progress had not been reached which justified the creation of corporations, and being in advance of commercial necessity, it was stamped as illegal, although the business involved was perfectly legitimate. It was sought to be carried out through the form of a trust, but neither the Courts nor the Statute condemned that form—they merely condemned the transaction because the age had not yet sanctioned stock certificates! The age had not yet learned to look upon the importance of transferring interests in industrial enterprises—one of the most important and necessary elements of commercial affairs — without which, to-day, the wheels of finance would be stopped. Mark the importance and interest of that case. The "trust" was not attacked — now the sole cause of discontent,—but the transferability of shares—now universally acquiesced in!

SECOND.—Combinations among victuallers or artificers, to raise the price of provisions, or any commodities, or the rate of labor, were also in many cases severely punished by particular statutes.* All of the Statutes were

* See 2 and 3 Edwd. VI., c. 15.

repealed as futile and contrary to the true commercial progress of England.

THIRD.—Monopolies were also attacked. Queen Elizabeth granted them, but in the beginning of the reign of James the First, Sir Edward Coke boldly and justly assaulted them, and in consequence a statute was passed in the same reign, declaring monopolies to be contrary to law and void.

The Queen granteth and the Parliament taketh away; and blessed is the name of that Parliament!

FOURTH.—I now call your attention to "Sir John Barnard's Act," which grew out of unhealthy speculations in stocks. After the East India Company had gotten under way, and the Bank of England was established, there was an enormous speculation in stocks, and Sir John Barnard's Act was passed for the purpose of preventing these speculations. Well, that act was to forever rid the English nation of the curse of speculation. A lovely and commendable purpose! But, alas! what was the result? Speculation increased. There was not a solitary conviction ever had under it, so far as I can ascertain, and it remained on the statute books down to the early part of the reign of the present Queen, when it was repealed, and I quote the preamble to the repealing clause to show what a confession the British Parliament was forced to make as to the inefficacy of such legislation.

> "Whereas an act was passed, in the seventh year of the reign of King George the Second, chapter eight, to prevent the practice of stock-jobbing, and by another act, passed in the tenth year of the said King's reign, chapter eight, the said first-mentioned act was made perpetual. *And whereas the said acts impose unnecessary restrictions on the making of contracts for the sale and transfer of public stocks and securities, and it is therefore expedient to repeal the same:* Be it enacted * * * the same are hereby repealed."

Statutes prohibiting stock speculation were also adopted in New York and Pennsylvania, but have long since been repealed, after lingering ineffectually upon the statute books. The law in New York, which was in existence from 1812 to 1858, without any deterrent effect upon the supposed evils it was passed to prevent, was not only repealed in the last named year, but the repealing law, recognizing the necessity of stock-trading, went further and absolutely legalized "short sales."

Speculations in Gold.

FIFTH.—The most notable example, however, of this species of legislation is to be found in this country, and it grew out of speculations in gold which caused an enormous agitation and excitement in Wall Street, as you, gentlemen, can remember from history, perhaps some of you personally. The effect and influence of the speculation in gold, it was thought, was so detrimental to the interests of this country, that Congress was invoked to pass a statute to prevent it, and it promptly did it; it passed a law in 1864, in June of that year, which you will find in the United States

Statutes, by which it was made a crime for persons to sell and deal in gold unless they were the owners of the coin.

Now, what was the effect of that statute? So absolutely ineffectual, futile and absurd was the legislation that gold went up thirty points the next day, and *fifteen days afterwards*, by the *same* Congress, the act was *repealed* because it was regarded as being absolutely detrimental to the interests of the country. Some enthusiasts, if you will call them by that mild name, bombarded Congress with the cry of legislation, and Congress succumbed into the arms of her new love, with the effect that gold advanced, and they repealed the law in fifteen days. A legitimate effect of legislating against the comet!

U. S. Anti-trust Law of 1890.

SIXTH.—Now, I bring you down to our own immediate legislation—what I call contemporaneous legislation—against aggregated capital, and I draw your attention again to the Federal Anti-trust Act of 1890.

That act was passed in 1890. I shall not analyze or discuss it. Why are you here? Why are you, gentlemen, sitting here and deliberating, when you have already on the statute books an act drawn by an astute statesman, which illegalizes all combinations, making it a misdemeanor to have combinations in restraint of trade? Why do you want more legislation? Is n't that statute enough? Can you find broader or more condemnatory language than that used in this Sherman Anti-trust Statute? If yea, how will you vary it, and what amendments will you make to that legislation, which will conform to the principles of Federal jurisprudence, and to the relation which this government bears to the different States?

Again, you have the States' statutes against "Trusts." I will not quote them. I merely recall them to your attention in this connection. Examine them, and you will see their inconsistencies; you will see how one State murders one industry, and encourages another; how one undertakes to separate labor from capital; pats agriculture on the back, and kicks industrials and manufactures.

These vast aggregations of labor, and aggregations of money, and aggregations of goods are in principle the same; you must not shrink from the responsibility that is upon you; if you determine that we must have more legislation, you must also legislate against, or at least in respect to, labor. Labor is, at least, as important as capital, and the man who undertakes to separate the two will involve and perplex this important economic subject. If it be wrong to combine industrials or aggregate capital, it is equally heinous to combine labor. They must each be restrained, or each have the fullest latitude of action. There can be no half-way, compromising measure.

And I also call your attention to another fact: there have been seven judicial decisions, at least, on questions of industrial combinations; we have had a decision in the Courts of New York which condemned the "Sugar Trust"; we have had one in Ohio which condemned the Standard Oil trust; the Biscuit trust has been declared illegal, and the Whiskey trust has been pronounced unlawful, and three others have been likewise condemned. Every time that these questions have come up before the Courts, they, on principles of common law, or by virtue of statute, or both, have declared these consolidations illegal. The Courts are clothed with ample power, under the common law rules of public policy and the doctrine of restraint of trade, to guard the interests of the public against combinations dangerous or hurtful to public interests. And yet how these so-called "trusts" thrive on adverse legislation and decisions! Every judgment of a Court pronouncing them illegal is the signal for the creation of more of the same kind.

And, therefore, I submit that no legislation is adequate to meet the new and, as yet, unknown quantity of industrial combinations. Exhaust the bountiful stock of law which you now have on hand, before you command a new supply.

Is Legislation Necessary to Regulate "Trusts"?

Are you here to fight against the mere *form* of things? If you are, I have wasted my time in appearing before you, and you have wasted yours in sitting here as a commission. Do you care what *form* aggregated capital assumes—whether it is in the *form* of the old common law trust, or whether it is in the *form* of a consolidation or a partnership or corporation? What is to be the result of this commission if you are to conclude that corporations may not *form a partnership* between themselves? what effect does that have on the question? If you legislate that all trusts, common law *trusts*, are illegal, that goes to the form. The *substance* of the transaction, be it remembered here, *means the extirpation of the carefully evolved commercial system of this country*, and it means nothing less. I say the fight against aggregated capital has so far been a vain fight against the mere *form*, and when it assumes a serious position, when it gets to a point that it means to earnestly attack the substance, then the contest will be to wipe out the commercial system of this country, and I ask if there is any man in this room, or any man in this country, who is ready to go to that extent? That is the proposition; I do not care whether you allow aggregated capital to exist in the *form* of a trust; I do not care whether you allow it to be in the *form* of a partnership or corporation; if it is bad, it is equally as bad in the last *form* as it is in the two others. And you are confronted with the question, if you mean to legislate, if you must legislate, of wiping out and extirpating a system under which this country has grown and developed and become as prosperous as it is, for without the corporations, without the power of combined financial action, we never would have reached the remarkable condition of commercial and physical prosperity which we now enjoy, to the envy of the balance of the world. Of course it is easy to remedy the supposed evils of aggregated capital. You can, if you are prepared to take such a step, wipe corporations from the statute books of this country, or so cripple them, by curtailing their inherent powers, as to make them impotent. But he is a bold man who will advocate such revolutionary measures. You can cut the throat of aggregated capital with the smallest knife of legislation; but who will commit the murder?

If corporations were bad, if aggregated capital were pernicious, if it distilled poison into the veins of the commerce and labor of this country, the time to have acted, if any action could be successful, was to have throttled the corporation in its cradle, forty years ago; but now, when it is entwined around every branch of our commercial development, its destruction means the end of our present commercial system, or it means a wretched, unseemly, in every way disastrous struggle between vindictive legislation and the natural law, which will still operate, however much it may be compelled to stoop to trick and evasion.

And in this connection we are brought

face to face with the question whether new legislation is required to regulate or destroy these new organizations. We are taught by men, who have made a study of those natural laws, which furnish the foundation for human legislation, that there are three things to be considered when new laws are to be made. The first is that you must consider the old law. What is the old law? Second, what is the mischief that the old law does not prevent? And third, what is the remedy proposed?

Now it is well settled that courts of equity possess the right to regulate or stop these commercial organizations or aggregations of capital when they are considered pernicious by virtue of the doctrine of public policy. Then we have the Sherman statute; you know its history. We have, in addition, the statutes of the various States, and you know their histories.

Here is a vast fund of equitable and statutory law upon which the public may draw in any emergency.

I ask, then, what is the mischief which is to be remedied? That is the question that this Commission must address itself to. Are you, to-day, satisfied that, since the inauguration of these industrials, they have been pernicious and detrimental to the people of this country? Can each member of this Commission put his hand upon his heart, and say, as a good citizen, that the records of this Commission are full of evidence which shows that these industrial enterprises are evil? Can you, in face of the extraordinary commercial development of this country, in face of existing favorable financial and industrial conditions, say that you are convinced that there are evils which spring from these industrials? If so, you must stop them. I claim to-day that there has not been a statement which an intelligent man could answer, pointing out in a specific manner the actual evils which have flowed from the inauguration of these enterprises. You say over-capitalization; well, that is a question of detail, that is a question about which men may possibly disagree. If you think that corporations should be capitalized upon the basis of the actual value, why, you will find a great many people who will agree with you. If you find, on the contrary, that they should be capitalized on the basis of the profits, you will find many more people who will agree with you. If you think this question should remain untouched, to be left with the parties themselves who are making the organizations, because you believe that this question of capitalization, one way or the other, is not a fundamental question, but is influenced and controlled by the operation of natural laws and of particular conditions, then leave it alone. But these are questions of detail; they do not go to the substance or root of this matter.

Perhaps it will be said that individuals have appeared before you who have suffered from aggregated capital. That may be true. The individual cases may be serious, they may be grievous, they may appeal to our sympathies, but, in the great progress of commercial development, some must go under, some must suffer, some must be crushed, and that has been an inevitable rule from the beginning of the world. If you had sat as a commission years ago, when the sewing machine was introduced, you would have had hundreds of supplicants coming before you asking legislation against it. Individuals do suffer and must suffer from the consequences of the general march of commercial and manufacturing progress. In that war of commercial development, the batteries of science and skill wound and kill their own countrymen and allies.

A great philosopher, Jeremy Bentham, was the author of the phrase, and the expounder of the great principle of, "The greatest good for the greatest number"—the only practical basis upon which you can successfully carry on government. Society is so constituted that some must suffer. It is the sacrifice, that the few are forced to make, for the good of the whole. Take the police and the school relation, in which you are interested. A man lives in a village, and has his own governess to teach his children, and also has his own man in the house; and he says to the authorities of the village: "You impose a tax on me for public schools; I don't need them, my children are taught at home; nor do I want your police; I have a man who performs that duty very well for me; I don't need the police and I will not pay the tax." Well, where does such a man stand? He must go down before the logic or argument of general good — the needs of the country require common schools, and they demand a police force. There is no principle of legislation that can be formulated without stepping upon the toes of some innocent people, who must suffer for the good of the whole. Undoubtedly some individuals—perhaps a great many—must suffer from the establishment of industrial combinations. The little grocer, the small haberdasher, the middleman, the salesman, the traveller, may have just cause of complaint, but the government is not made to adjust these things or to remedy such evils. We are not living in the millennium. We are not governed by abstractions, nor is the State influenced by sympathy. These are cruel facts, but no less inevitable than that the sparks fly upwards.

I do not mean to assert to you, gentlemen, that aggregated capital is an unmitigated virtue, without accompanying vices. What I have been endeavoring to impress upon you is the necessity of going slowly in your acts. I have been endeavoring, by invoking historical analogies, to show you how easy it is to make laws, and that the fruits of hasty legislation not only bring the courts of justice and the administration of the law into reproach, if not to say contempt, but fail to accomplish the purpose at which the legislation is aimed.

Now, what can more forcibly illustrate the strength of that remark than the anti-trust law of the United States? I do not suppose that the author of that law ever conceived the idea or intention of affecting by that piece of legislation the railroad interests of the country. And yet we have this remarkable result, that the industrial and manufacturing corporations, as contra-distinguished from railroad corporations, have escaped the law, as we see in the case of Knight*, the sugar refining case from Philadelphia, where the United States Supreme Court held that, although the effect of combining sugar refining businesses created a monopoly in the manufacture of a necessary of life, yet it could not be suppressed under the Sherman Act of 1890, because it was not a restraint of interstate trade or commerce.

But, strange to say, the railroad corporations, which, I think, were not intended to be embraced in the law, were made the sufferers by that legislation! And in the two decisions, in the Missouri case, and in the freight cases about which you know, to the reports of which I need not refer, the Supreme Court held that the language of the Act of

* 156 U. S. Reports, 1.

1890 applied to railroads, and contracts which were generally conceded to be fair and beneficial to the public were set aside as illegal. I have no criticism to make of these decisions. But see the paradoxical result! A scheme of legislation, which aimed at manufacturing and industrial corporations, is declared not applicable to them, and railroad corporations, which were not intended to be covered, are held to be within the language and spirit of the statute! He must be a wise man and a good lawyer to draw a statute, and both of these characters are scarce to-day.

Evils of Trusts.

I do not claim here that there are not great and grave questions surrounding the aggregation of capital, in any form it may assume, whether it is held by an individual, a partnership, or a corporation. It is a matter of profound solicitude to every citizen of this country, a matter of profound importance in the development of this country, in all its operations, but I say that the subject has not approached a ripe and mature condition. I say that if you take the vague, indefinite and crude thoughts which up to this time characterize the discussion of this question, and put them in the crucible of legislation, nothing tangible, practical and beneficial to the people will come from the experiment. That is all. You must keep your eyes upon this modern octopus, whether it is in individual or corporate form, but until aggregated capital commits some indisputable blow against the liberties of the people, until it strikes at the foundation of our institutions, or until it interferes with the administration of justice or legislation in some positive way, I say that it is futile and unnecessary to enact any laws, because you have no defined, fixed, intelligent purpose in view, and without such purpose you are absolutely at sea, and the very laws that you make will strike at people whom you never contemplated they would reach, and probably, if not certainly, permit the aggregations of capital, intended to be embraced, to entirely escape.

It may be that the effects of combinations,

or the effects of the aggregation of wealth or capital, may produce corruption in the legislative and judicial powers of the government. There is the great danger, in my opinion. But no law that you can frame can reach this supposed evil by anticipation, because you do not know what form it may take. For direct corruption, the existing penal laws of the Nation and the States are amply sufficient, and need nothing in the form of fresh laws.

Judicial or legislative corruption, however, is often provoked by demagogism, which presses corporations to seek for their just rights by illegitimate means. It is a public saying, unfortunately, in this country, that no corporation can get proper and necessary privileges without a lobby. I wish you, gentlemen, to ponder deeply over that aspect of the question. A corporation goes to a municipal legislative body, and wishes a certain privilege, which, if granted, will benefit the public, yet the railroad men, and the men who control corporations, will tell you that it cannot be obtained by legitimate methods. Now, there is no need to disguise the fact that occult influences are used sometimes by large corporations, of necessity, to obtain things which are of the greatest importance to the public, and if you can stop that end of it, you remove one great temptation to judicial or legislative corruption.

If demagogism is eliminated from the discussion of these questions of aggregated capital, there is no doubt that a solution will be found entirely satisfactory to the true progress and interests of the country.

In concluding this branch permit me to repeat, that it appears to me that all we have to-day to found legislation upon is the opinions of men who are not qualified to speak with any intelligent authority; we have the vague and indefinite criticisms of people who have not studied these questions from the standpoint of actual experience or the honest conviction resulting from deep research. Whenever these critics appear before this Commission, if they dare do so, you will insist upon proof, upon statistics, upon real argument and facts, and you will then have a basis upon which you can build the foundation for a law which will be satisfactory to all.

[NOTE.—Prof. J. W. Jenks, the Expert Agent of the United States Industrial Commission, who, as he says, spent twelve years in the personal investigation of the "Trust Problems" and kindred subjects, cautiously specifies under eight different heads the evils which *may* result from consolidations of capital. He says:

> "(1) Investors of capital are often grievously wronged through concealment of facts and deception practised by promoters and directors at the time an industry is organized, and, later, through misrepresentation of the condition of business and of the methods in which a business is carried on."

Happily, the law furnishes adequate and ample remedy to the investor who is inveigled into buying securities by false representations or concealment of material facts, the *suggestio falsi* or the *suppressio veri.*

> "(2) A second class of persons injured is that of the stockholders. Directors not infrequently manage the business in their own interests, regardless of those of the stockholders. At times it is really made less profitable, or is so managed as apparently to be less profitable, in order to depress the stock on the market and to enable the directors through gambling speculations to reap large profits."

Full redress is given to stockholders for the above wrongs. They have the power, through the Courts, to compel the directors or trustees to account for any loss which results to the stockholders by reason of the mismanagement or fraud of the directors. There is nothing in this statement of grievances that is not capable of being redressed by present laws.

"(3) Persons, not members of a corporation, *may be* injured as consumers by high prices, which can be kept high, provided the combination *can secure monopolistic* power. The temptation to keep prices above former competitive rates is, of course, greatly increased when the corporation has issued large amounts of watered stock."

These grievances must be left to be corrected by natural conditions. The securing and exercising of real monopolistic power, except when resulting from patents, can always be remedied by the Courts, which have power, when a real monopoly is made out, of stopping it.

"(4) The producers of raw material *may be* injured by low prices, which the combination, by virtue of its being the largest, if not almost the sole buyer, can compel the producer to accept."

No fact is given to support this hypothetical injury. The learned professor's statement is purely supposititious, and no evidence is produced to show that any such consequence has followed. But such a situation can be safely left to natural conditions.

"(5) The combination *may* so increase its power as to injure the wage-earners by compelling them to accept lower wages, or to work under less favorable conditions, than would be granted by competing concerns. So, too, the power exercised, apparently arbitrarily at times, of closing part of the plants to avert a strike, or even to affect the stock market, is dangerous."

This is also hypothetical, and no evidence is adduced to show that such conditions as are described ever existed. They may exist, and if they do, the right of labor to combine to prevent them, is undisputed.

"(6) It *may* happen at times that the larger organizations will exert so powerful an influence on our political organizations that the purpose of the State will be directed away from the common weal."

This possibility has already been adverted to by me [p. 100]. It is an important element in the question of the development of aggregated capital, and it must be carefully watched by the people. The learned Professor suggests no remedy for the possible evil.

> "(7) The *mental* tone of the business community *may be* lowered by depriving individuals of the privilege and of the power to enter independently into business as readily as could be done were capital less concentrated. It should be borne in mind that this evil, while it exists, is offset, in part, by some of the advantages mentioned above."

This, again, is hypothetical, and until some real case is presented, the situation must be left to the operation of natural laws.

> "(8) And, again, the *moral* tone of business *may be* lowered. If the larger organizations employ unscrupulous methods in dealing with competitors, or customers, or laborers, their greater power, especially if it is great enough to give them a partial or complete monopoly for a time, will have a much more detrimemental influence than the same acts of an individual, both on account of the range of its application and of the more powerful influence of its example."

But no remedy is suggested to reach this possible evil when it arrives, and it must be assumed that it is thrown out merely as a warning note to persons who are seriously studying these problems.

"A reasonable degree of publicity regarding both the organization and management" of corporations is advocated; but at the same time caution is advised in the making of any laws.

Thus after twelve years of personal experience we have one single remedy suggested by Professor Jenks—that of publicity! A sweeping comment upon the drastic remedies proposed by politicians and political platforms! And yet, in a day, evils may be revealed as flowing from these aggregations, which would require remedies even beyond those suggested by demagogues bidding for temporary fame and political capital.]

Federal or State Legislation.

Assuming that you, gentlemen, should come to the conclusion that some further law was necessary, you are confronted with a question as to the jurisdiction; as to whether it should be a National or State law. This involves some study as to the nature of our government, and the true relation of the States to it. This government is a federative government with national functions. Whatever powers this federative government has are given to it by the Constitution. The Constitution of the United States may be divided under two great heads—namely, that part which we carried almost bodily from the English law, and that part which was created to uphold the federation.

If you will take occasion to study this great instrument, you will find that the expressions of individual rights in Magna Charta are almost copied in the Constitution of the United States. And if you examine the three foundations of the English government to-day, the Magna Charta, the Petition of Right and the Bill of Rights, you will discover that all of our rules of liberty, justice and right, State and National, have been drawn from these sources. Whatever is new in our Constitution is the result of the association of the thirteen States, by which they agreed, for the purpose of mutual and perpetual union, to delegate to a general government certain specified powers.

The idea of the Constitution of the United States was that the general government should never interfere with any of the reserved internal affairs of the States. The government wanted just power enough to protect itself from the exterior influences, and to hold the States together, and it did not propose to interfere with the rights of the States to govern themselves as to their internal affairs, any more than the respective States undertook to interfere in the domestic relations or private affairs of any of its citizens.

If you keep that idea in mind, you can intelligently approach the question whether the Federal Government has the right to interfere in the general questions of aggregated capital.

The necessity for some such provision, as the present "commerce clause" in the Constitution, was one of the controlling causes for calling the convention, which led to the adoption of that instrument. When we separated from England, the great difficulty was the want of uniformity, in the commerce and navigation laws.

In the Articles of Confederation, which preceded the Constitution of the United States, there was nothing which made commerce free, open and uniform, between the States; and when they received their independence, the question of an untrammelled commercial intercourse, between the States of the Union, was one of the principal subjects which confronted the people. That clause of the Constitution of the United States by which Congress was given the power to regulate commerce—I say this with great confidence—was never intended as an absolute authority for the general government to interfere or meddle with the internal affairs of the States.

The phrase "*regulate* commerce" does not mean to *restrain* commerce, and never was intended to have such meaning. In placing this language in the Constitution there was no thought of interfering with the development of the country. The framers only undertook to say this: that the States should not deprive each other of that free and absolute intercourse between themselves which must necessarily exist for the purpose of accomplishing the purposes of the Union. That was the intention. They said all of the navigable waters must be open to all the States; no impediments placed in the great highways and roads, and no restrictions made upon trade and commerce as between them. The citizens of South Carolina, so far as the navigable waters and roads, and everything that appertained to commerce, were concerned, should enjoy the same equalities and privileges that a citizen of New York possessed.

In the first case which arose in the Supreme Court of the United States, Gibbons *vs.* Ogden,* under this commerce clause of the Constitution, the question was this: Livingstone and Fulton, who were then applying steam to water navigation, had received from the Legislature of New York, a grant for the exclusive use of steam, in the navigable waters of New York State, for a term of years. Well, that was a privilege that nobody envied them in receiving; because Livingstone and Fulton were applying a new and great discovery to the propulsion of boats, and the State gave them the sole privilege of enjoying this valuable invention. But they had no sooner obtained this grant from the State of New York, than another individual, started a line of steamboats from New Jersey, and ran over to New York, and he was seized. He was under a license of the United States Government, regulating

* 9 Wheaton's Rep., 1.

the coasting trade, and the question arose in the Supreme Court of the United States, whether the State of New York had the power to grant such an exclusive privilege, to the exclusion of citizens of other States navigating under coasting licenses. The opinion of Chief Justice Marshall, delivered in this case, has been universally read and studied, and he held, that it was one of the objects, of the commerce clause of the Constitution, to open the navigable waters, to all citizens of other States, and that the grant to Livingstone and Fulton was inoperative.

"The genius and character of the whole government seem to be that its action is to be applied to all the external concerns of the nation, and to those internal concerns which affect the States generally; but not to those which are completely within a particular State, which do not affect other States, and with which it is not necessary to interfere for the purpose of executing some of the general powers of the government. The completely internal commerce of a State, then, may be considered as reserved for the State itself."

This language of Chief Justice Marshall furnishes the keynote to this much discussed clause of the Constitution.

Of course, the Supreme Court of the United States—I say it with great regret—has been remarkably harassed and annoyed in its decisions upon this clause. I do not think any man can sit down and study the decisions of that Court upon the interstate commerce clause, without rising from the reading, with a feeling that they are very inconsistent in some respects; and Judge Bradley, in one of his decisions *—and certainly Judge Bradley was a very able lawyer—expressed a regret that the Court had strayed so far away from the principles of Gibbons *vs.* Ogden, from which I have just quoted.

The judges of the Supreme Court of the United States are human, and they are more or less susceptible to the influence of outside opinion, and discussion, as others are. Law, after all, is nothing but the expression

* Leloup *vs.* Mobile, 127 U. S. Rep., 640.

of custom. Despite the fact that legislatures undertake to put in statutory form, laws for the government of the people—that which is the great law, and that which is the universal law, is the law of custom; and the Supreme Court judges, like all other human beings, are susceptible to the influences that prevail at the time they write their decisions—honest, high-toned, intelligent, proud of their position in every way, but still human, as you can see, if you take the Legal Tender cases, where they made two decisions, one in favor of legal tenders, and one against them, and if you take the Income Tax cases, and other instances—few, I am glad to say—you will see that that Court is influenced very largely by the prevailing popular opinion. They breathe the same air, they live under the same influences as other people do; and when a question of law is presented there, they are susceptible, more or less, to the atmosphere which prevails, and everybody must recognize that indisputable human frailty.

I say, therefore, that Congress should not put upon that Court unnecessary burdens, as they have done by the Sherman Act. It was a crude piece of legislation at best, and that Court has endeavored, in an honorable and conscientious way, to extricate itself from it, as much as it can; but it would have been much better, in my judgment, if that law had never been enacted, because it unnecessarily attempts to deprive the States of power which they alone should exercise; it is another innovation of the general government—it is another unnecessary step towards centralization.

Gentlemen, the strict State rights doctrine has been largely obscured since the war of 1861, because many issues, **State Rights.** which were involved in it, disappeared, when that unhappy epoch in our history closed.

But the subject, of the relation of the Federal Government to the States, is still one of the profoundest importance, and it should always be kept alive and green, before us, when legislation, of the kind involved in this discussion, is contemplated.

I do not assert these views as the result of political and partisan bias, but they are influenced by independent thought and conviction. As Mr. Gladstone says, if we can preserve it, as it has been handed down to us, there is not "the slightest doubt about our political equality and our progress and development."

State rights is not a party question. It has disappeared from the realm of partisan politics, and when you are inquiring into the legality of business carried on by manufacturing corporations incorporated under State laws, and the question of restricting or limiting them, you must be warned not to encroach upon the authority of the various States; and it is very important, that conscientious study should be bestowed upon this important subject, before Federal legislation is granted. It is unfortunately true, that lately we are tending to nationalization. It is true, that in great and small emergencies, people are turning to the National Government for help, for assistance and support; but it is equally true, in my humble judgment, that such appeals should be disregarded, and that the fabric of this Government never can be sustained in its pristine vigor and glory unless we keep the identity of the State Governments perfectly established, as against the Federal power. And now that that great bone of contention, slavery, has disappeared, we have a chance to look at the question, from an independent and unbiassed standpoint, uninfluenced by sectional or partisan politics.

The question of State rights involves the whole theory of our Government, and the perpetuation of our republican institutions. It is essential, in considering the subject of making laws, to endeavor at all times to maintain the individual autonomy of citizenship. We begin with the household, family and domestic affairs, and we say to the village, or town, or city, or State, whichever undertakes to invade the privacy of these relations, "You must keep your hands off." As citizen members of villages, towns, cities or municipalities, we claim the general right to legislate for ourselves, with only so much interference from the State as is necessary for the general good of the whole people, and when we come to State citizenship, we claim that the Federal Government has no power over us, except that which has been delegated to it by the Constitution. In any legislation inaugurated by the Federal Government, it is, therefore, essential that there should be no encroachment upon the rights of the States, as they are preserved in the Constitution. In State legislation, as against municipalities, cities, towns and villages, it is equally important that the rights of these smaller communities should not be invaded, and the same reasoning applies to the invasion of individual, domestic, family or business affairs, by the National or State Government, or by any of the minor municipalities.

Looking at the subject, therefore, in the

light of every fact, which I have been able to discover, I see no reason why there should be any national legislation in respect to this question of aggregated capital.

In regard to State legislation, you are charged with suggesting a basis for homogeneity of laws upon this subject. Nothing appeals to me so strongly as that proposition. The draftsman of the act, which created your Commission, had in view the possibility of your reaching a conclusion upon which you could not conscientiously recommend national legislation; but he has carefully given you the power to make recommendations by which homogeneity on this subject between all the States could be established—similar laws framed on the same line; the States to take up this great question and legislate in a uniform way. A recommendation, emanating from this Commission, ought to have the profoundest weight in all the States, especially if it is accompanied by reasoning which appeals to intelligent men.

If such a homogeneity can be obtained, I will not dwell here upon its profound political significance, as tending to a community of interests and legislation between the people of all the States, and thereby sinking still deeper the foundations of that kind of "union" contemplated by the framers of the Constitution.

Therefore, I submit that if you recommend legislation at all, it can only be in the shape of proposals to the different States. And if it is true that any corporation in this country—I do not care which corporation it is—is in possession of franchises, or is in possession of rights, or is the holder of privileges which are not granted to or enjoyed by other corporations or individuals, then I say if you are satisfied of that fact, level your legislation against it specifically, and do it clearly, and the people will applaud you, and the courts can intelligently sustain you.

As I see the subject, without having the whole light before me as you have, sitting here patiently, as you have been, for months, and gathering in all the statistics, facts and opinions, it seems to me that the legal remedies, in the various States, are ample to-day to redress all grievances which may exist, and about which I now wish to talk.

Existing Remedies Applicable to Corporations Analyzed.

There are three classes of persons who are interested in the remedies appertaining to aggregations of capital; first there is the Public; second, the State; and thirdly, the creditors and stockholders.

Now, let me first take up the question of the Public. There has been much talk, and it has received sanction from the very respectable authority of Judge Howe, in his formulation of the results of the Chicago Trust Conference held in the summer of 1899; there is a strong demand in favor of more publicity in respect to these industrial corporations.

Well, let us inquire what interest the Public has in, what I shall now term, corporate wealth and corporate interests. The Public—

and I mean by the Public those persons who have no pecuniary or contractual interest in the corporation—is that class of persons who are interested in corporations, solely and because corporations are created by public statutes, and whose interests cannot extend beyond knowing that the corporation is faithful to its charter—to its obligations to the State.

I take issue with the advocates of publicity here, and I deny that it is necessary in the broad sense in which it is demanded. I say that no man who is not interested in a corporation has a right to know anything about it. It is none of his business. I put that proposition very boldly. I may be wrong, but my views are definite—subject to change, but at this time well fixed. I repeat that if you guard the rights of stockholders and persons who have contractual relations with corporations, and the State continues its paramount authority over the corporations—as I shall show you it possesses—and the corporation keeps its contract with the State by strictly following its charter; then, and in such events, the public has no more business in its private concerns than it has in the private affairs of your household, or your fortune, or your own commercial affairs.

The line between the exercise of governmental rights—now I am speaking as if the State were offering to make a law controlling corporations—I say that the questions as to where and when the State should legislate, and where and when it should not; as to when private rights intervene, and the State should withdraw; where the State's right to intervene, and the private rights must yield; are questions of the greatest delicacy. And I do not know that I can do better than to quote to you from Mr. Burke, who, in my opinion, is an authority on any subject which he has touched, at any time, and in any place. But it is clear, that when you come to the question as to whether the State shall legislate about what concerns your domestic or business relations, I say, unless the necessity is overwhelming, it ought to keep its hands off. You ought to allow the autonomy of household affairs, and the autonomy of business, to exist in accordance with the wishes of the individuals who are interested in it; and the Government has no more right to interfere with your business than it has to go into your house and ask you what you are eating, or to dictate what you shall eat. The line between where the State or Government comes in, and where the citizen ought to be supreme, is clearly put by Mr. Burke.*

"It is one of the finest problems in legislation," says Mr. Burke, "and what has often engaged my thoughts whilst I followed that profession, 'what the State ought to take upon itself to direct by the public wisdom, and what it ought to leave, with as little interference as possible, to individual discretion.' Nothing, certainly, can be laid down on the subject that will not admit of exceptions, many permanent, some occasional. But the clearest line of distinction which I could draw, whilst I had my chalk to draw any line, was this; that the State ought to confine itself to what regards the State,

* Burke on the Features and Details of Scarcity, at page 416. Rivington Edition of 1808.

or the creatures of the State, namely, the exterior establishment of its religion; its magistracy; its revenue; its military force by sea and land; the corporations that owe their existence to its fiat [this phrase undoubtedly means public corporations, as private corporations were not, at the time this was written, in existence]; in a word, to everything that is truly and properly public, to the public peace, to the public safety, to the public order, to the public prosperity. In its preventive police, it ought to be sparing of its efforts and to employ means, rather few, frequent and strong, than many, and frequent and, of course as they multiply their puny politic race, and dwindle, small and feeble. . . . They ought to know the different departments of things; what belongs to laws, and what manners alone can regulate. To these, great politicians may give a leaning, but they cannot give a law."

Now there are a great many things that the State has no right to regulate. There are a great many things that the State has no right to go into at all; about which it has no right to dictate. It has no right to dictate to me what religion I shall follow, what I shall eat, what I shall wear or what business I shall engage in. Mark you, I do not lay down this as an absolute proposition, an unqualified one; what I mean is this, that unless there is some overwhelming necessity, some apparent and powerful moving cause and mischief at hand, the State should keep its hands off, that is what I mean. But if the mischief is plain; if you feel that overwhelming cause forcing itself upon you, then you are justified in legislation, and you will find plenty of authority for it, under the police power and under every other power.

I come back, then, to the question of publicity, and I assert that the public is amply protected by existing laws. So far as the general public is concerned, if it is influenced or damaged or defrauded by any act of a corporation, or its directors, or its promoters, or anybody associated with the enterprise, there is a criminal and a civil legal remedy, full, complete and absolute. Let me illustrate: If a corporation were to issue a circular, a prospectus, which is now becoming the method of introducing new organizations to the public and getting subscriptions—if there is put in that prospectus, any statement which is false and fraudulent, it is a foundation for a criminal indictment. Here is a perfect remedy, existing under the laws of every State in the Union. You do not have to guard the public in that respect. No excuse can be found in this respect for the intervention of the State. If a man puts his money into a corporation through the representations contained in the prospectus, he has a civil remedy for damages in addition to his criminal remedy. So that there is no possibility of anybody being defrauded, or cajoled, or influenced, out of his money rights or property, by anything that the corporation, or any of its surrounding associates, or persons interested in it, can do, without an appropriate, full and perfect remedy.

I am dealing now with the outside public, before they get into the corporation; and I affirm that it is utterly impossible for you to conceive of a case, where the public is swindled, or where the public loses money, by corporate action, unless there are adequate civil and criminal remedies. Whether they are enforced or not is another question. Now, so much for the public.

If the solicitude of those opponents of aggregated capital is based on the fact that they wish to protect the public, then I say to them that the public is amply protected; they can wish no further protection. A superabundance of laws upon the same subject confuses rights, it does not aid their enforcement. I admit that men have been, are and will continue to be swindled, fleeced, deceived or mistaken in their speculations and investments in stocks. But the State cannot give its citizens brains and judgment to guide them in these matters. Therefore much of the talk about publicity is purely Utopian.

Now, let us go a step further. Take the stockholder: what are his rights? The stockholder of a corporation has the absolute right to open the books. You need no law on that subject. The directors of a corporation are trustees for the stockholders, and the books of the corporation can be opened to them, through the instrumentality of a court of equity, under the powers that a court of equity inherently possesses, or a court of common law, or under statutory power, at any reasonable time after any reasonable demand. Their rights are fully protected, and while there may be isolated cases, where stockholders have failed to get at the books, if you will examine the cases, you will discover the grounds of the failure. Persons sometimes buy stock for speculative objects, for the purpose of finding out what is going on in a certain corporation, and for no other motive. Lord Ellenborough said to a man who was in court, in the case which I cited from East's Reports, "You have not clean hands; you came into this suit speculatively; you have bought into this corporation for the purpose of making this examination"; and in such instances as these the courts refuse to allow examinations of corporate books to be made. But every *bona fide* holder of stock has the right to open the books of the corporation, and every court in this country will aid him to do it, and if they do not—if there is anything incomplete in the remedy in that respect—I say make it so; it ought to be so; but if you study the question, I say that you will be satisfied that a complete remedy already exists. If you want homogeneity in the rules of the different States, that is another matter.

Therefore, so far as the stockholder is concerned, his rights are amply protected at law or in equity.

Now, let us come to the State. Here is where the principal question arises, and I will not differ, with the most radical exponent of the doctrines of anti-aggregation of capital upon this question. The State is the creator of the corporation. The State dictates the terms upon which the corporate charter is granted. The charter makes the corporation a *quasi* public body. The State has the absolute right, not only to make examinations, but it has the right to extinguish the charter, as you would extinguish the flame of a candle. It can destroy the life of a corporation at any moment; because the condition in the Constitution of all the States now is that the States reserve the right to revoke all charters. Not only that, but the State has, what we call in equity, a visitatorial power. It has the power through its attorney-general of visiting a corporation, inquiring into its methods of doing business, and making a thorough examination of its books, and of its accounts and its business, if sufficient justification exists to warrant such a course. So that the States are not deficient in power; and the cry of publicity, in my estimation, is entirely unwarranted by the law and facts. But if you were to make a law by which the whole public could pass through the office of a corporation, and look at its affairs, as you would pass through a street and look through the windows into an office, to discover what was going on there—I say that such a license, to the general public, would be infringing the rights of the corporation—it would be

9

infringing individual rights; you would be guilty of transcending the power of government, unless you had, as I say, some overwhelming, powerful, good, substantial motive to do it. With the law as it is to-day, giving the State transcendental powers over corporations, protecting stockholders and creditors, and the public as well, I believe that the cry of publicity has no foundation to rest upon.

Should Corporations be Prohibited?

Now, one more thought. Some persons, I think, have an idea that these aggregations of capital should be extinguished —wiped out. They make a warfare against capital, and their aim is apparently to exterminate it as something offensive to the smell, to the eye, and to the touch—something repulsive to the senses, something which should be blotted out of existence, as unholy and pernicious, and vile and evil. Gentlemen, where will such legislation lead to? Have the opponents of capital reflected upon the consequences of such an act? Certainly they have not, or they would not for one moment dream of legislation of that kind. Why, who constitute the corporations, and where would such legislation lead? Legislating against corporations! You are legislating against yourselves. To-day every large corporation in this country has thousands of stockholders, and every substantial blow aimed against corporations is a blow aimed against the middlemen, the men of small means, the conservative men, the thousands and thousands of stockholders who have invested their money in these corporations, the young and old, the widow and the infant, the trustee and the executor. Do these people imagine for one instant that they strike a blow at the millionaire in battering down corporations? Will they succeed in stripping these great millionaires of their wealth when they legislate against corporations? Never! The millionaires can take care of themselves, and do it. They do not hold their millions and millions of dollars in these large corporations. And when you hear of this banking house, or that banking house, taking ten or fifteen or twenty millions of dollars of bonds or stocks, why, it only means that it is the source through which the stock and bonds reach the public.

The great banking interests, the great promoters of these commercial enterprises, retain but comparatively small interests in these colossal industrial corporations, and when legislation is made against them, remember that you are striking at your fellow-citizens whom you are meeting every day; the man of conservative wealth, or the man who has put his little savings into corporations to enable him to support his wife and children. It is a cruel mistake, not to say blunder, to discuss these questions upon the lines of wiping out capital and exterminating it. It is as senseless as impossible.

One more thought and I shall close. In connection with this crusade against aggre-

The Influences and Necessity of Protecting Wealth.

gated capital it is fashionable to cry out against individual wealth. There is not in the political history of this country any appeal so demagogic, unnatural, unfounded and unsustainable as that which is made against wealth. The instinct of envy, or the worst passions of prejudice, or demagogism and ignorance, lie at the base of such appeals. That you and I have not been fortunate enough to accumulate wealth, is no reason why we should undertake to criticise, and find fault with, those who have gotten it legitimately, much less to seek to deprive them of it.

Respect for the goods and property of others is the basis of human society. It is demanded by social duty; it is inspired by good manners; it is inculcated by divine rule; and should be rigidly enforced by civil law and authority. The professional agitators in this country should understand, that the free and unlimited opportunities, inducements and openings of business and wealth to its individual citizens, constitute one of the strongest arguments in favor of a republic, and are at the same time its main foundations. The incentive to wealth is an honorable and useful ambition for the citizens of any government to possess, because acquisition of wealth requires intelligence, shrewdness, conservatism, self-denial and the exercise of all those human and moral qualities and functions which are beneficial to society. It is a primary object of every well-founded government to encourage the acquisition of individual fortunes, as it is one of its most sacred duties to guard them for its possessors when they have been lawfully and honestly earned. To encourage men to toil and labor, in all the fields of human industry, means the development and prosperity of the nation; it means the opening of new fields of occupation to the poor, needy and unemployed; it encourages men to tremendous and sometimes superhuman efforts of skill and energy. The consciousness that the rewards they reap as the result of their own exertions, whether in money or in any other kind of property, will be carefully guarded by the state for their own benefit and the benefit of their posterity, is the great motive which impels men to strive mightily in the different fields of business activity. Nor should wealth be driven from an active participation in the political life of the nation. As a matter of right and justice and policy, it should have its proper place in the councils of the government.

As Mr. Lecky * says:

> "The indissoluble connection of the enjoyment and dignity of property with the discharge of public duties was the pre-eminent merit of feudalism, and it is one of the special excellencies of English institutions that they have in a great measure preserved this connection, notwithstanding the necessary dissolution of the feudal system."

It constitutes one of the greatest elements of stability, conservatism and intelligence, and while I have the contempt that is shared by most of my fellow-citizens for the ostentatious display of fortunes, the flaunting of wealth before the public with brutal vulgarity, I do contend that most of the individuals

* Lecky's *History*, England in the Eighteenth Century.

who have acquired wealth in this country, are entitled to be respected, and it is not only their right, but it is their duty to insist upon exercising a fair and proper share in the government of the country. The road to fortune is open to us all, and if we have not individually been successful enough to acquire a great amount of property, we should not seek to belittle the men who have been more fortunate, or to seek in any way to deprive them of it, or diminish its importance or enjoyment. The lives and achievements of the men who have acquired wealth in this country form one of the most interesting chapters of history. Who are the men who occupy the elegant residences on Fifth Avenue, and on other avenues of the great cities of the country? Not men who were born into the world with large means; but men who from their infancy were thrown out upon their own resources, and by hard work, skill and luck, have acquired fortunes. It should be a matter of pride, to point out these men, as types of American citizenship, and as proper incentives to young people of the present age. Any onslaught, premeditated or otherwise, made upon the property of such a class of people, is not only senseless and ridiculous, but aims at the whole root of the social organization.

The American nation is neither in its decline, nor in its dotage. Men may climb into prominence, on the steps of temporary argument, and unfounded appeals to passion and prejudice. Demagogism may temporarily capture the multitude, but the American people cannot always be deceived. Those who seek to allure the laboring and agricultural classes, or others, into the approval of schemes which have not the sanction of good sense, history, judgment and constitutional law, will sooner or later come to grief.

THE EVOLUTION OF CAPITALISM

Allen, Zachariah. **The Practical Tourist,** Or Sketches of the State of the Useful Arts, and of Society, Scenery, &c. &c. in Great-Britain, France and Holland. Providence, R.I., 1832. Two volumes in one.

Bridge, James Howard. **The Inside History of the Carnegie Steel Company:** A Romance of Millions. New York, 1903.

Brodrick, J[ames]. **The Economic Morals of the Jesuits:** An Answer to Dr. H. M. Robertson. London, 1934.

Burlamaqui, J[ean-] J[acques]. **The Principles of Natural and Politic Law.** Cambridge, Mass., 1807. Two volumes in one.

Capitalism and Fascism: Three Right-Wing Tracts, 1937-1941. New York, 1972.

Corey, Lewis. **The Decline of American Capitalism.** New York, 1934.

[Court, Pieter de la]. **The True Interest and Political Maxims, of the Republic of Holland.** Written by that Great Statesman and Patriot, John de Witt. To which is prefixed, (never before printed) Historical Memoirs of the Illustrious Brothers Cornelius and John de Witt, by John Campbell. London, 1746.

Dos Passos, John R. **Commercial Trusts:** The Growth and Rights of Aggregated Capital. An Argument Delivered Before the Industrial Commission at Washington, D.C., December 12, 1899. New York, 1901.

Fanfani, Amintore. **Catholicism, Protestantism and Capitalism.** London, 1935.

Gaskell, P[eter]. **The Manufacturing Population of England**: Its Moral, Social, and Physical Conditions, and the Changes Which Have Arisen From the Use of Steam Machinery; With an Examination of Infant Labour. London, 1833.

Göhre, Paul. **Three Months in a Workshop**: A Practical Study. London, 1895.

Greeley, Horace. **Essays Designed to Elucidate the Science of Political Economy,** While Serving to Explain and Defend the Policy of Protection to Home Industry, As a System of National Cooperation for the Elevation of Labor. Boston, 1870.

Grotius, Hugo. **The Freedom of the Seas,** Or, The Right Which Belongs to the Dutch to Take Part in the East Indian Trade. Translated with Revision of the Latin Text of 1633 by Ralph Van Deman Magoffin. New York, 1916.

Hadley, Arthur Twining. **Economics**: An Account of the Relations Between Private Property and Public Welfare. New York, 1896.

Knight, Charles. **Capital and Labour;** Including *The Results of Machinery*. London, 1845.

de Malynes, Gerrard. **Englands View, in the Unmasking of Two Paradoxes**: With a Replication unto the Answer of Maister John Bodine. London, 1603. New Introduction by Mark Silk.

Marquand, H. A. **The Dynamics of Industrial Combination.** London, 1931.

Mercantilist Views of Trade and Monopoly: Four Essays, 1645-1720. New York, 1972.

Morrison, C[harles]. **An Essay on the Relations Between Labour and Capital.** London, 1854.

Nicholson, J. Shield. **The Effects of Machinery on Wages.** London, 1892.

One Hundred Years' Progress of the United States: With an Appendix Entitled Marvels That Our Grandchildren Will See; or, One Hundred Years' Progress in the Future. By Eminent Literary Men, Who Have Made the Subjects on Which They Have Written Their Special Study. Hartford, Conn., 1870.

The Poetry of Industry: Two Literary Reactions to the Industrial Revolution, 1755/1757. New York, 1972.

Pre-Capitalist Economic Thought: Three Modern Interpretations. New York, 1972.

Promoting Prosperity: Two Eighteenth Century Tracts. New York, 1972.

Proudhon, P[ierre-] J[oseph]. **System of Economical Contradictions:** Or, The Philosophy of Misery. (Reprinted from *The Works of P. J. Proudhon,* Vol. IV, Part I.) Translated by Benj. R. Tucker. Boston, 1888.

Religious Attitudes Toward Usury: Two Early Polemics. New York, 1972.

Roscher, William. **Principles of Political Economy.** New York, 1878. Two volumes in one.

Scoville, Warren C. **Revolution in Glassmaking:** Entrepreneurship and Technological Change in the American Industry, 1880-1920. Cambridge, Mass., 1948.

Selden, John. **Of the Dominion, Or, Ownership of the Sea.** Written at First in Latin, and Entituled *Mare Clausum.* Translated by Marchamont Nedham. London, 1652.

Senior, Nassau W. **Industrial Efficiency and Social Economy.** Original Manuscript Arranged and Edited by S. Leon Levy. New York, 1928. Revised Preface by S. Leon Levy. Two volumes in one.

Spann, Othmar. **The History of Economics.** Translated from the 19th German Edition by Eden and Cedar Paul. New York, 1930.

The Usury Debate After Adam Smith: Two Nineteenth Century Essays. New York, 1972. New Introduction by Mark Silk.

The Usury Debate in the Seventeenth Century: Three Arguments. New York, 1972.

Varga, E[ugen]. **Twentieth Century Capitalism.** Translated from the Russian by George H. Hanna. Moscow, [1964].

Young, Arthur. **Arthur Young on Industry and Economics:** Being Excerpts from Arthur Young's Observations on the State of Manufactures and His Economic Opinions on Problems Related to Contemporary Industry in England. Arranged by Elizabeth Pinney Hunt. Bryn Mawr, Pa., 1926.